SPIRITUAL ASTROLOGY AND THE WISDOM OF THE AGES

SPIRITUAL ASTROLOGY AND THE WISDOM OF THE AGES

A Quest for Self-Improvement

Alexis J. Stephanou

Edited by Emilie Hunter

VANTAGE PRESS
New York

Excerpts from the Dhammapada are reprinted by permission of the
Theosophy Company.

FIRST EDITION

All rights reserved, including the right of
reproduction in whole or in part in any form.

Copyright © 1992 by Alexis J. Stephanou

Published by Vantage Press, Inc.
516 West 34th Street, New York, New York 10001

Manufactured in the United States of America
ISBN: 0-533-09528-X

Library of Congress Catalog Card No.: 91-90802

0 9 8 7 6 5 4 3 2 1

Contents

Preface

The purpose of this book is to share with the reader the knowledge that I have gained from my teacher, Zoltan S. Mason, of New York City. It is through his insight into astrology that I have undergone a spiritual awakening.

Although philosophy and metaphysics in general had fascinated me since adolescence, my interest in astrology specifically did not come until rather late in life, primarily because my career in the public sector and foreign service of my country, Greece, did not leave me with the time necessary to explore new fields. Just before my career in the foreign service was due to come to an end, I was in New York for a session of the United Nations General Assembly. Almost by chance, I went to Mason's Bookshop, a metaphysical bookshop on Lexington Avenue in New York City, and there I met its owner, Zoltan S. Mason. I paid several subsequent visits to the Bookshop, but it was not until three years later that I asked Mr. Mason, who is a well-known astrologer, to set up my horoscope. With his sound judgement, tremendous life experience, and deep knowledge, not only of astrology and metaphysics, but also of human nature, he made an interpretation and assessment of my horoscope that was very direct and challenging for me. I was (1) to be active lifelong dealing with the public; (2) to survive the hard times to come, both physically and psychologically; and (3) to study matters connected with the human soul.

Since I was in New York just for a short time and unsure of whether I would come back (and if so, how often), I made up my mind to attend the astrology classes given by Zoltan Mason as frequently as my duties at the United Nations would allow.

From the very first lesson, I was impressed by Zoltan Mason's teaching method. His mind and intellectual range were the outcome of a perfectionistic self-training. He provided an excellent example for me of someone who, with much hard work and self-discipline, had successfully trained himself.

I had never in my life met a teacher whose approach to a subject so complex was so down-to-earth and yet at the same time so full of the purest metaphysical speculations. From the very first lecture I attended onwards, I took notes.

Whenever I was back in New York, I tried not to miss any of Mr. Mason's lectures and was, luckily, able to attend most of them, thus confirming the saying that "when the *shellah* is ready the guru will appear." Fortunately, opportunities for me to come to New York increased. Whether this was merely a coincidence, or rather a sign of destiny, is for the reader to decide.

Mr. Mason's references to the Bible, Oriental wisdom, various philosophers and ancient astrologers motivated me to search further into these areas. During the course of my readings, I found that both my memory and my intuition became unexpectedly coordinated; I discovered at propitious times quotations and thoughts that corresponded to the astrology lessons. Never before had I such encouraging experiences as these, which Ralph Waldo Emerson, in another context, would have called "both stimulating to emotions and inspiring to the intellect."

Zoltan Mason's lectures were intended for those desiring to become astrologers. I tried to arrange my class notes in textbook form, realizing at the same time the difficulty in conveying to the reader the practical guidance of the lessons and their deeper message, since many of the lessons dealt with the spiritual aspect of astrology.

It had not occurred to me that the trends or events forecast from a horoscope could be so closely connected to the wisdom of the ages and to the world at large. This revelation I owe to Zoltan Mason. I am grateful to him also because he gave answers (to the questions I posed during his lessons) that were always remarkable in that they had such a broad scope. The lessons have given me more than knowledge of astrology; they have brought a source of inspiration for the rediscovery of treasures forgotten or diluted by men in present times.

Some parts of this book are repetitious. This is intentional. A few of the illustrating examples may look prosaic, but I wish to remind the reader that life must not be viewed in fragments, rather as a whole. The serious student should never overlook the spiritual quest hidden in astrology.

Finally, I will quote a most enlightening passage from an article by Saul Bellow (*New York Times Book Review*, March 8, 1987), titled "The Civilized Barbarian Reader." It illustrates so vividly why people would do better to revert to "the other sciences" that are not taught in schools and that could better assist them in solving their larger problems:

> To finish with *Herzog*, I meant the novel to show how little strength "higher education" had to offer a troubled man. In the end he is aware that

he has had no education in the conduct of life (at the university, who was there to teach him how to deal with his erotic needs, with women, with family matters?) and he returns, in game language, to square one—or as I put it to myself while writing the book, to some primal point of balance.*

With this book having just been completed, Saul Bellow's article came at a time as if to justify my new endeavors.

* Reprinted by permission of Saul Bellow.

Acknowledgements

I want to express my sincere thanks to my astrology teacher, Zoltan S. Mason, of New York City, without whom this book would not have come into being, since its text contains parts of the astrological lectures given by Mr. Mason between 1983 and 1988. I have great respect and admiration for his knowledge, judgement, and keen insight into human psychology and behaviour. Zoltan S. Mason is an astrologer of tremendous experience, compassionate, ethical, and humanitarian. He is a rare human being.

I am especially indebted to my wife, Lydia, who, during her brief and only stay in New York City in 1980, discovered, due to her longstanding interest in astrology, Zoltan Mason's bookshop. I am also obliged to a precious friend, the late Marion von Cramm, who, in 1983, informed me of Mr. Mason's lectures.

I am indebted to Emilie Hunter, the editor of this book, for her fine help and advice, which made publication possible. I am most grateful to her.

Last, I would like to acknowledge Hassan Jaffer of Toronto, Canada, who, from his first examination of my horoscope, conveyed to me his certitude that I would write books in the latter part of my life.

♈	ARIES
♉	TAURUS
♊	GEMINI
♋	CANCER
♌	LEO
♍	VIRGO
♎	LIBRA
♏	SCORPIO
♐	SAGITTARIUS
♑	CAPRICORN
♒	AQUARIUS
♓	PISCES

☉	SUN
☽	MOON
☿	MERCURY
♀	VENUS
♂	MARS
♃	JUPITER
♄	SATURN
♅	URANUS
♆	NEPTUNE
♇	PLUTO
☊	NORTH NODE OF MOON

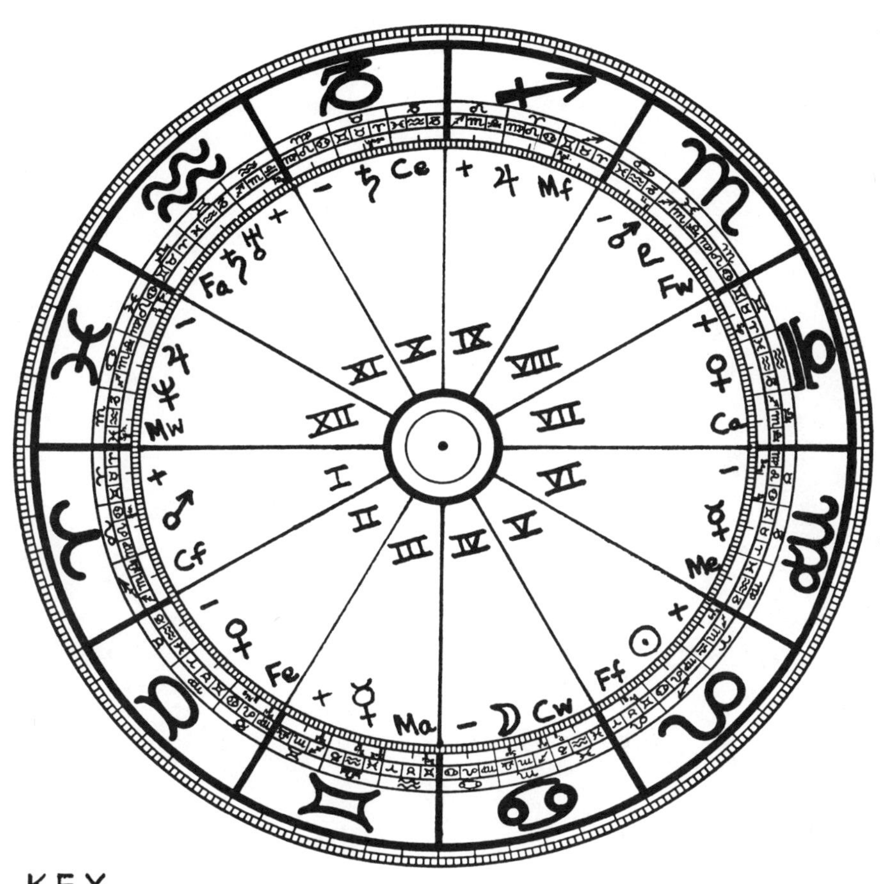

KEY

+	MALE
-	FEMALE
C	CARDINAL
F	FIXED
M	MUTABLE
f	FIRE
e	EARTH
a	AIR
w	WATER

Introduction

Astrology is the logic and the language of the stars. It is not an exact science. Astrology is based on observation and judgement and is a tool to help others. An astrologer must understand human nature ("Judge not thy neighbour until thou art in his place") and have an insight into the problems of life. He should be diplomatic. Astrology should be in the hands of spiritually strong people, whose duty is to help and not to harm. A person who does not love mankind cannot become an astrologer.

There are four rules that an astrologer should follow: the first is to be discreet; the second is not to harm or destroy; the third is to help through advice (an astrologer has to think carefully of the way in which he should formulate his advice, because the way in which a problem is solved by his advice is important); and the fourth rule is to achieve the interpretation of the horoscope.

Astrology requires the ability to synthesize. The more one's fantasy and imagination work, the better the chance one has of a good interpretation.

Each of us is driven by the zodiac and his own horoscope. The astrologer should ask himself how much he should influence his clients, so as not to take away too much of their free will. An astrologer should also be careful not to increase the problems and anxieties of his clients. At the time an astrologer begins to study a horoscope for the first time, he must have in his mind not only the horoscope in question, but also that of his own and of the archetypal zodiac. The archetypal zodiac reflects the general, and a given horoscope the particular.

Even though it is impossible to know the details of a person's past from the horoscope alone, an astrologer should always focus on what the horoscope shows, and thereby determine why the enquirer asks for his judgement. He should not go by what the enquirer tells him, since people are usually poor judges of themselves, and what they say may, or may not, be true or accurate. Childhood experiences are not necessarily important.

The individual with an evolved horoscope may raise questions that the horoscope, by itself, cannot answer. The reply of the astrologer should take into consideration the reason the questions were raised. As a rule, people do not speak openly. An astrologer must sense how the person receives the planetary influences. Is he an optimist or a pessimist? If a pessimist, how can he be made to become optimistic? Sometimes this can be achieved simply through a positive interpretation of the horoscope by the astrologer. One should not go through life with too much pessimism. (If one wants to become an astrologer, one had better learn to smile.) Optimism is wisdom. Whatever you do or advise, remember that extremes are bad. On examining a birth chart, one's first task is to find what is missing, so that the enquirer may be advised how to overcome the deficiency or disharmony in his (or her) horoscope. The examination of the horoscope is done in three steps. The first is to examine the houses, the second is to examine the signs, and the third is to examine the planets, in that order.

The key to understanding a horoscope is knowing how to combine its elements correctly.

If one has a problem, he should work it out in his profession. Astrology enables one to detect his abilities for a profession. Through the Tenth House (the house of realization and destiny), one can solve many problems. Never ask for solutions too soon, however. One's energy should be used for the constructive buildup of a profession.

There are two ways of seeing astrology: either as a deep philosophy that explains the meaning of life, or as representing laws of nature that cannot be deceived or by-passed. Human beings do not understand these laws well enough at their present stage of evolution.

The wise astrologer will be ethical and will make a clear distinction between ethics and morals. Ethics result from wisdom and the laws of nature. Morals reflect the laws of the community. FYSIS KAI NOMOS: "NATURE AND LAW," the phrase of the ancient Greek sophists, indicates the distinction between the laws of nature and the laws of the community.

> Do not be confined to this world but be transformed by the renewal of your mind, that you may prove what is the will of God, what is good and acceptable and perfect.
>
> —Romans 2:12

It is ethical to be in harmony with the laws of nature and to find the right quantity (measure) and quality. An ethical person does not interfere negatively with another individual.

The true student of astrology will not deal in childish predictions. He will determine the way in which planetary influences are received by the enquirer and how much the free will of the person can change these influences. Learning how to react in a positive way to our own birth charts is the ultimate achievement. It is very important to know the zodiac, for through it, one can find hidden powers that become active.

With the zodiac being the archetype, the ideal, whatever in a birth chart is a duplication of the zodiac should be considered desirable.

It is a great art to be able to decipher the zodiac, but to decipher it completely is impossible, because we can never arrive at the first mover (primum mobile), or God. This remains a secret. There are secrets in life. No scientist can understand the universe completely. However, the search for the primum mobile is the ultimate search.

> As you do not know how the spirit comes to the bones in the womb of a woman with child so you do not know the work of God who makes everything.
>
> —Ecclesiastes 11:5

> The wind blows where it wills, and you hear the sound of it, but you don't know whence it comes or wither it goes; so it is with everyone who is born of the Spirit.
>
> —John 3:8–9

The tree of knowledge is forbidden. In astrology, the tree (knowledge) is represented by Mercury. The opposite is wisdom, which is represented by Jupiter. Here are some examples of the wisdom of Jupiter: "We are not entitled to discriminate"; "One must see the two ways or sides"; "Life is synthesis." The first step in the search for the primum mobile is to depart from the earth (the ascendant in a horoscope) and to proceed to the planets, which are senders and receivers of influences.

To create means to give life. We give life to meanings. For example, each word has a meaning on three different planes: the physical plane, the conscious plane, and the unconscious plane.

> Words without thoughts never to Heaven go.
>
> —*Hamlet*, Shakespeare

> Fancy is a notion devoid of any real basis and following upon knowledge conveyed by words.
>
> —Patanjali, Book I:9

xvii

A lot depends upon thinking correctly.

Nature is male and female, active and reactive. The first law of nature is polarization. Nothing can exist without its opposite. Basically, the active and the passive must be united. There is equality at one point: the center.

The motion that activates the perpetual circle, symbolized by the snake devouring its tail in ancient Greek mythology, is seen also in the sequence of signs of the archetype (the zodiac). Motion can be toward either evolution or involution.

Evolution brings one to a higher state of mind, from an earthly approach to a spiritual approach. The spirit represents the highest in us. The purpose of one's present incarnation is to arrive, through trials and experiences, at this higher state of mind. Life is very hard and to be able to evolve, one has to fight.

Involution indicates the need for the instincts to be directed by the will (the Sun) towards a purpose that could prepare one for a spiritual approach.

The nameless unites everything, which in Buddhism is reflected by the word ZEN.

Every master who practices an art molded by Zen is like a flash of lightning, from the cloud of all-encompassing Truth. This Truth is present in the free movement of his Spirit and he meets it again in 'It', as his own original nameless essence. . . . If he (every master) is irresistibly driven towards this goal, he must set out in his way again, take the road to the artless art. He must dare to leap into Origin so as to live by the Truth and in the Truth, like one who has become one with it.

—*Zen in the Art of Archery*
Eugene Herrigel

The truth is what appeals to our reason. The search for truth helps produce clarity of thought, healthy emotions and purity of aspiration.

Him I call Brahamana whose speech is truthful, gentle, instructive, which offends no one.

—The Dhammapada:
The Brahamana 26 (408)

The truth is always veiled (as in the veil of ISIS). Truth often hurts. If the full truth is unveiled (known) to a person, he will die.

I have yet many things to say to you, but you cannot bear them now. When the Spirit of Truth comes, he will guide you into all the truth.

—John 16:12,13

Truth is different for different persons. Each of us is born to fulfill a task. Each chooses his own path in life. We are not here to answer all questions. Man is not perfect. Truth has twelve faces, as seen in the twelve signs of the zodiac.

To each is given the manifestation of the Spirit for the common good.

—1 Corinthians 12:7

But each one has his own special gift from God, one of one kind and one of another.

—1 Corinthians 7:7

As long as we are here on earth, we must aim to be healthy in body and spirit. Each one should perceive his horoscope correctly. A person with a good horoscope should not be afraid of life or of death. Our health is affected by our thoughts. We have to discard every negative thought or idea, since it will have a destructive effect. (We should also remember that we hurt ourselves by overdoing.)

Argue your case with your neighbour himself, and do not disclose another's secret.

—Proverbs 25:9

The Judeo-Christian religions are built upon guilt and anxiety. Pessimism and spirituality do not go together. Religion should result in optimism. Pessimism destroys.

For God is not a God of confusion but of peace.

—1 Corinthians 14:33

The spiritual man does not worry. Anxieties should disappear because they develop conflicts.

I want you to be free from anxieties.

—1 Corinthians 7:32

A good astrologer must be able to answer questions both to soluble problems, such as those connected with the profession, and to insoluble problems arising from the emotions. An astrologer should point out the advantageous qualities in a person's horoscope that are relevant for a profession. Just as all professions need dedication, so astrology needs dedication.

Every horoscope has a purpose. Everything in a horoscope must be integrated. A truly integrated horoscope is the one that could lead a person to the highest development that can be pictured astrologically. Each person expresses his own horoscope. The task should be to perfect one's present expression. The greatest knowledge is based on the integration of one's own horoscope.

A basic problem is in determining what is the right measure and what is superfluous, for even an excess of goodness can be harmful. When is enough, enough? Even philosophers cannot give an answer to this question. The only way to find the right measure is to apply the right thinking. Everything is based upon the right thinking. Right thinking comes when one works for other people, when one knows the personalities of others, and when one has a great understanding of life. A person who understands life is cheerful. "To understand everything is to forgive everything." "Forgiveness is the key to resolve any problem." Right thinking will prevent you from suffering.

Cheerfulness is very important for an evolved person and will improve his karma.

> Each one must do as he has made up his mind, not reluctantly or under compulsion, for God loves a cheerful giver.
>
> —2 Corinthians 9:7

People should be encouraged to develop not only cheerfulness, but also self-confidence, and to get rid of shyness and the fear of making mistakes. To overcome shyness, you must learn to be completely independent from what others do or say. You have to learn how to react to social pressure.

> For God did not give us a spirit of timidity but a spirit of power and love and self-control.
>
> —2 Timothy 1:7

> They blame him who sits silent,
> they blame him who talks much,

they blame him who speaks moderately
in measured terms.

—The Dhammapada: Anger 7(227)

A man is happy if luckily he escapes the sight of fools.

—The Dhammapada: Happiness 10(206)

Religions teach that one should not have a negative self-image.

There are two approaches to astrology; the healthy one, which decreases superstition, and the unhealthy one, which increases superstition. One should build up something in a healthy way. To build up mental health, be optimistic by remembering that no matter how gloomy things get, there will always be sunny days again!

The most difficult thing to obtain is good judgement, and astrology requires excellent judgement. For it, you need an excellent Moon (for the unconscious), a good Mercury (for an analytical mind), and a good Jupiter (for synthesis). Experience is obtained with great pain, but we have to gain experience in order to shape our own futures.

A horoscope is a combination of the sky (the signs) and of the earth (the houses). Everything in the sky is good. The sky represents wisdom: it has its own values. In the sky, all problems are solved.

In order to understand human nature, you have to remember that every part of it has its specific function. The knowledge of another human being is possible only when you know yourself.

Seldom do people understand love. Love can involve suffering, but if you truly love, you don't suffer. If one loves, one gives, and aims to make another person happy. In marriage, how much should one have to tolerate in order to make the marriage a happy one? That will depend on the personality of the partners. In a marital relationship, a person with discernment does not influence his partner. You marry somebody in order to bring into your life what is missing. A happy marriage implies harmony between two people. (Can there be harmony between two people? The answer is "yes.")

If you are evolved spiritually, no sign of the zodiac will harm you. "Live and let live." In order to marry happily, you must be intelligent, an optimist, and a giver. To be independent may prove to be impractical. Wisdom must include the understanding of the personalities of other people. The longer you are unmarried, the more you are inclined to go towards your own ego. Marriage can be a way out of melancholia. Nature is both male and female, but a man cannot completely know a woman,

xxi

and a woman cannot completely know a man. Society is male-oriented. Even though men are not scheming, women must protect themselves from men.

The true secret of life must be found in the unconscious. Since most events come from the unconscious (the Moon), the will (the Sun) is not always used. Human beings are imperfect, so the purpose of life may be to achieve greater perfection, and to get rid of anxiety.

We have to be humble and must not fight for vanity and nothingness.

—Ecclesiastes

The fear of the Lord is instruction in wisdom, and humility goes before honour.

—Proverbs 15:33

To fear the Lord is to hate evil, hate pride and arrogance, evil behaviour and perverse speech.

—Proverbs 8:13

The unconscious is more important than the conscious, because one's drive comes from the unconscious. The study of astrology can assist us in the evolution of the unconscious. If the unconscious is well developed, the solutions to one's problems will be in his dreams. Dreams are the spontaneous manifestation of the unconscious. It would be beneficial if we could learn to bring dreams to our conscious, making the right interpretation of the symbols that appear in them, but, if we are not sufficiently evolved, there is a danger in knowing our unconscious because it is ugly, bearing the instincts of an animal. You would be surprised if you were truly to know your unconscious. It is because the unconscious (the soul or Moon) is dangerous that we need the conscious (the spirit or Sun) to direct it. The soul has to be realized in a civilized way with the help of the Sun. When the conscious does not work, we call it insanity. Nowadays, people tend to suppress the unconscious.

The planet Saturn is considered the Guardian of the Threshold (between the conscious and the unconscious). It brings foresight. However, too much foresight can lead to anxiety, and too much anxiety can lead to neurosis. With the latter case, the psychoanalyst can achieve a catharsis by removing the Guardian of the Threshold. Like astrology, psychoanalysis has to do with people's unconscious. There is a certain amount of danger in all professions that delve into the unconscious.

xxii

We have to find our own methods of making anxieties disappear. We are not limited in this respect. The best defense is to go away from the earth toward the sky for spiritual evolution, i.e., to aim for a higher state of mind. One must never give up hope. One must preserve hope within himself and within others. We can overcome our difficulties. However, it is more easily achieved with a male ascendant, because the conscious (male) is stronger than the unconscious (female) and gives motivation for activity.

The astrologer may detect the future behaviour of an individual from his horoscope.

The purpose of spiritual astrology is to know more about the secrets of life and nature. True astrology is a deep philosophy that attempts to explain the meaning of life. Analysis of life is fruitless, because life is synthesis. Wisdom is to recognize this synthesis.

The answer as to whether planetary influences can be modified is "yes." Perfection is possible. Planets influence us according to the way in which we receive their influence (in a positive way or in a negative way). Can spiritual evolution be detected? The answer should be "yes, but only partly."

And which of you by being anxious can add one cubit to his span of life?

—Matthew 7:27

I know your works; you have the name of being alive, and you are dead.

—Revelation 3:1

If you will not awake, I will come like a thief, and you will not know at what time I will come upon you.

—Revelation 3:3

One has to be dedicated in life. Indifference is a curse. One must choose a healthy environment in which to live; in particular, people who are oversensitive should choose their environments very carefully, because, by being emotional, they can easily become afraid of their environments. Can one's environment change the way he receives planetary influences? The answer is "Yes, to some degree." The right environment for an astrologer is the one in which he can find intellectuality and people interested in metaphysics. A hermit has no environment.

Ascetism wrongly practised leads downward to hell.

Alas, the ascetic scatters more and more the dust of his passion.

—The Dhammapada: The Downward Course 6, 8 (311–313)

One has to persevere and to enhance one's will. One of the most difficult things for a teacher to develop is the will power of his students.

And as for that in the good soil, they are those who, hearing the word, hold it fast in an honest and good heart, and bring forth fruit with patience.

—Luke 8:15

They who fear when there is no cause for fear and they do not fear when they ought to fear—both enter the downward path following false doctrines.

—The Dhammapada: The Downward Course 12(317)

According to Hillel, if you don't increase your knowledge, you automatically decrease it. Scepticism and pessimism can lead to a morbid state of mind.

According to Hermes Trismegistus, there is possibility for wisdom.

Each human being is both a sender and a receiver of influences. We receive influences from the planets and we, in turn, send out influences. For example, one can influence the unconscious of another person by his voice. The voice of a human being is very important. (The Mercurial voice is high in pitch, the Venusian voice is melodious, and the Martian voice is forceful.)

The planets are transmitters. They receive influences from the zodiac. With regard to the zodiac, they are receivers and are reactive and feminine in nature. With regard to the Earth, the planets are senders, and are active and masculine in nature.

The signs of the zodiac are senders, but how beneficial a sign is depends upon how one receives the influence. The signs are more important than the planets, but human beings can receive influences from the signs only through the planets, which are the transmitters. The signs cannot exist for us without the planets. The signs are manifested in the lines on the palms of people's hands and the planets in the lines of their foreheads.

The birth chart shows the desires of a person.

Desire is the dwelling upon pleasure.

—Patanjali, Book I:7

The desires change according to age, so a person's age will provide the key to his desires. The idea of the general versus the idea of the particular changes with age. There are seven ages in a human life. One of the reasons that no society can be completely healthy is because of the discrepancy of conflicting desires, which vary according to age groups and to the social and ethnic environment.

The Ten Commandments may be summarized thus: "Don't do it. If you do it, you are going to be punished." Whatever evil we do, we pay for.

Take precautions before the evil appears; regulate things before disorder has begun.

—TAO TE KING: Paradoxes

According to the Old Testament, people washed themselves when they didn't feel completely pure:

Wash yourselves; make yourselves clean; remove the evil of your doings from before my eyes; cease to do evil, learn to do good; seek justice, correct oppression; defend the fatherless, plead for the widow.

—Isaiah 1:16–17

We are unaware of the radiations that we, as human beings, transmit. One of the concepts in spiritual astrology is that there are vibrations more subtle than most of us realize. One should endeavour to be more receptive to these subtle vibrations. Color and music have influences on the human mind and body. They possess subtle vibrations of their own. Spiritual astrology teaches us to conceive the world differently. The physical body is perceived within the context of the conscious and the unconscious. The more you evolve, the more you emanate radiations.

Wise men must communicate. Wise men lay up knowledge.

—Proverbs 10:14

The tongues of the wise dispense knowledge.

—Proverbs 16:2

xxv

What are the laws of nature? The first law of nature is survival (self-preservation), the second is the survival of the race, and the third is not to cut oneself off from the influence of God. Anxiety is not in harmony with the rules of nature.

We must fulfil our horoscopes. If we follow the right path, we cannot fail. One's values will depend on his age group. The most important planet is that associated with one's age group, because it determines the way in which he receives the planetary influences.

We can communicate by providing examples to others. A person should communicate his evolution by giving a good example.

Virtue lasting in old age is happiness.

—The Dhammapada: The Elephant 14(333)

Happiness is the outcome of good conduct.

—The Dhammapada: Evil Conduct 3(118)

Do your best to present yourself to God as one approved, a workman who does not need to be ashamed and who correctly handles the word of truth.

—2 Timothy 2:15

For a young man, Saturn (time) is the greatest enemy. For an old man, Saturn is a friend, because during his life he has had the opportunity to adjust himself to the time element. Time is the only thing we cannot fight.

All things do their work, and then we see them subside. When they have reached their bloom, each returns to its origin. Returning to their origin means rest or fulfilment of destiny.

—TAO TE KING: TAO as a moral principle, or "virtue"

What is important for a human being is his drive. A person will become successful if he maintains a strong drive throughout his life. One's drive should go from one's ascendant (the Earth) to one's Tenth House (the house of profession and destiny). Having no goal means weakness. If somebody is weak, he cannot take disharmony, which makes survival more difficult. In our civilized society, disharmony prevails. The unprepared person cannot survive well either.

The unconscious desires (the instincts) are more important than the conscious desires, since one's drives come from the unconscious. The unconscious drive is that of survival and procreation. To follow necessity is the key to survival. The urge to stay alive is the most important; it is a healthy instinct. As soon as it vanishes in a person, he or she becomes unimportant. The strongest drive comes from the fire signs. Watery signs, representing emotions, take away this drive. Whatever has to do with the emotions represents difficulties. Emotional problems result from ignorance, egoism, desire, and aversion.

Aversion is the dwelling upon pain.

—Patanjali, Book I:8

One must work against bad instincts, i.e., those that cannot be directed by the Sun (the will) towards a purpose that is advantageous and to realize them in a civilized way. If the instincts are realized in the wrong way, it is highly dangerous. One can change a lot through self-education. One can become independent of one's unconscious through Raja Yoga, Zen Buddhism, and autogenic training (Karma Yoga). The power of the conscious must be increased, but it must continue to influence the unconscious. The Sun masters the instincts and gets rid of anxieties.

Whenever the Moon is in Capricorn, there is anxiety and, generally, because Capricorn is an earthy sign, melancholia. Anxiety is connected with Saturn and the Moon.

You have to find a way for the will to work on all levels in order to open the door to a higher perception. Sanity and self-respect should be maintained. The will (the Sun) can be increased through patience (Saturn). Patience is the greatest manifestation of the will. With patience, one can work against interferences and realize one's goals. If you achieve your horoscope in the right way, you will be rewarded, and what you achieved will be maintained.

Help is provided either by a fortunate horoscope or through events (trials, pain, suffering). Jupiter protects. Venus, the planet of love, is a helper. Neptune represents all love, i.e., love on a higher level, love that does not discriminate. Love has become difficult to find in today's world.

Mankind benefits if you give a good example, but remember, you are responsible only for yourself. Our present task is to perfect our present expression. If you want to help others, help yourself first.

If I am not for myself alone, what then am I? And if not now, then when?
—Hillel

One must become his own helper.

Let no one neglect his own good work for the sake of another's, however great. Once a man has discerned his own work let him devote himself to it.

—The Dhammapada: The Self 10(166)

Purity and impurity belong to oneself. No man can purify another.

—The Dhammapada: The Self 9(165)

Some people, in order to change, escape reality.

A person must improve himself before he can attempt to do good works in the world, and self-improvement comes through action.

We have to show that we are fearless, self-confident, and cheerful.

Do not be afraid of sudden panic or of the ruin of the wicked when it comes, for the Lord will be confidence and will keep your foot from being caught.

—Proverbs 3:25,26

Overprotection is a form of fear. To protect oneself is good, but to overprotect shows anxiety.

You will keep in perfect peace him whose mind is steadfast, because he trusts in you.

—Isaiah 26:3

In order to serve others as part of the community, one must in the beginning isolate oneself from the community so one can meditate and determine one's goals.

Let each man first establish himself in the way he should go and then let him teach others. Thus the wise man will not suffer.

—The Dhammapada: The Self 2(158)

Albert Schweitzer said that the strongest man is the one who serves others.

We cannot live for ourselves alone, but must come to realize that there is

xxviii

no such thing as separateness, and no possibility of escaping from the collective karma of the race to which one belongs, and then, we must think and act in accordance with such belief.

—William Q. Judge
New York, October 1890
Antecedent words to the *Bhagavad-Gita*

I know your works; you are neither cold, nor hot. Would that you were cold or hot! So, because you are lukewarm, and neither cold nor hot, I will spew you out of my mouth.

—Revelation 3:15,16

We must serve others by setting a good example and by being sincere with ourselves. To this effect, we need a certain kind of courage, without which we will not be able to admit limitations; a sustained purity of aspiration is also required.

Each person can find his mission in life by examining in his own horoscope: first, the ascendant (calculated from the time of birth, which is based on the first intake of breath); second, the Moon; third, the Sun; and fourth, whatever is unusual. (The position of the Moon in the birthchart represents the horizon at the time of conception.) A horoscope is bad when the survival instinct is not strong. One must study the signs in which the ascendant, the mid-heaven, and the ruler of the ascendant are. Look at the planets that are connected with the ascendant and the mid-heaven, as well as the houses where those planets are. The influence of the planets is received through the rising sign. Remember that the Moon and the Earth receive influences, and that the Sun realizes the Moon.

The training of a positive character involves depth of thought, patience, stability, and a happy disposition.

Action is of two kinds: first that accompanied by anticipation of consequences; second that which is without the anticipation of consequences.

—Patanjali, Book III:23

He who is steadfast in righteousness will live, but he who pursues evil will die.

—Proverbs 11:19

Therefore everyone who hears these words of mine and puts them into
practice is like a wise man who builds his house on the rock.

—Matthew 7:24

Solid rock is not shaken by the gale. The wise man is not moved by praise
or blame.

—The Dhammapada: The Wise Man 6(81)

Goodness can have its own perversions caused by:

a) **excess** (even an excess of goodness can be harmful):

Extreme straightness is as bad as crookedness.

—TAO TE KING: *Paradoxes*

A wise man is cautious and turns away from evil, but a fool throws off
restraint and is careless.

—Proverbs 14:16

b) **deficiency**:

What was sown on rocky places is the man who hears the word and at once
receives it with joy but since he has no root, he lasts only a short time.

—Matthew 13:20

Evil tendencies of the unrestrained and careless go on increasing if they
neglect doing what ought to be done and do that which ought not to be
done.

—The Dhammapada: Miscellaneous 3(292)

c) **inadequate use of higher, beneficial forces**:

In everything a prudent man acts with knowledge, but a fool flaunts his
folly.

—Proverbs 13:15

In the blaze of prosperity, his virtues were insensibly tinctured with the adjacent vices: justice with cruelty, liberality with profusion, desire of fame with puerile ostentatious vanity.

—Gibbon, "Rienzi," *The Decline of the Roman Empire*

And we may learn from the example of Cato that a character of pure and inflexible virtue is the most apt to be misled by prejudice, to be heated by enthusiasm and to confound private enmities with public justice.

—Gibbon, ibid.

The disciple of Plato might exaggerate the infirmities of nature and the imperfection of society.

—Gibbon, ibid.

Stimulation is necessary in the training of a negative character, in order to improve it. It is better to fail than not to struggle at all.

Negative tendencies are caused from mental inertia, various subtle forms of stubbornness, selfishness, and lack of aspiration. These can be indicated by a Saturn that is afflicted by a bad aspect from Mercury, Jupiter and/or Neptune.

We can get rid of afflictions by meditation which implies concentration. The practical part of concentration: establishing meditation and eliminating afflictions. The true enemies of concentration are sickness, languor, doubt, carelessness, laziness, addiction to the object of sense, erroneous perception, failure to attain any state of abstraction, instability in any state when attained.

—Patanjali, Book I:30

All spiritual leaders should retire at some stage of their evolution in order to escape from the human environment, and to consult the sky.

For the Lord your God goes with you: He will never leave you nor forsake you.

—Deuteronomy 31:6

The battle refers . . . also to the struggle which is inevitable as soon as any one unit in the human family resolves to allow his higher nature to govern him in his life. Hence, bearing in mind the suggestion made by Subba Row (learned Brahmin Theosophist: Notes on the Bhagavad-Gita), we see that Arjuna, called NARA, represents not only Man as a race but also any individual who resolves upon the task of developing his better nature.

xxxi

What is described as happening in the poem to him will come to every such individual; opposition from friends and from all the habits he has acquired, and also that which arises from hereditary tendencies, will confront him, and then it will depend upon how he listens to Krishna, who is the Logos shining within, and speaking within. Whether he will succeed or fail.

—William Q. Judge
New York, October 1890
Antecedent words to the *Bhagavad-Gita*

You cannot solve your problems unconsciously. You solve your problems consciously through your actions. For a profession, cardinal signs and harmonious aspects between the Tenth (career), the Second (money), and the Sixth (employees) houses are helpful.

SPIRITUAL ASTROLOGY AND THE WISDOM OF THE AGES

Fate and Destiny versus Free Will

Fate, also called destiny, or predestination, negates free will. The ancients believed strongly in fate. Muslims believe that fate is Allah's decision and that the future cannot be changed. With fate there is no way out. A fatalistic attitude should be considered a dangerous attitude. If you accept the expression "fate," you will fail. One way to free oneself from fate is through the TAO of the Chinese.

Western astrology is less connected with the idea of fate than is Eastern astrology, e.g., Hindu astrology. According to many philosophers, fate (Moira) can be changed through will power, but how much this is possible cannot be determined through astrology. Sometimes nature goes against the expression of human will if the latter has been overextended. One should always remember that: "Many are the plans in the mind of man, but it is the purpose of the Lord that will be established" (Prov. 18:21).

There is a German saying that human beings should not challenge the gods. There are limits that are not always necessarily identifiable and quantifiable. The question will always be "How far can we go against our destinies?"

It is very difficult to judge when enough is enough, but the quality of fate can be changed. It is a discipline that belongs to DHAM-MAPADAH, the teachings of Gautama Buddha.

"Character is destiny." Through psychological training one can change the way one receives planetary influences and increase or decrease the influence of a planet, thus modifying fate to an undetermined extent. As to the question "Is there fate?" the answer is that fate exists to a very strong degree, but intelligence may interfere with it. Even one's diet may change one's fate. Physicians may interfere with fate, and science interferes with, and continuously fights it. Today, medicine, science, and civilization can interfere with our destinies and so we must consider the influences of the sky in connection with free will and the possibility that free will has increased as a result of the advances in technology and medicine.

The right approach to astrology is to use it to understand one's own destiny. One must realize that everything has a purpose. The Tenth

House is connected with one's destiny. A good astrologer can decipher the human destiny in any horoscope.

As to the question whether or not one's predestination can be changed, the answer is that one has the possibility to make his destiny better or worse for himself. One can upgrade or downgrade his destiny.

Exceedingly hard it is to do that which is beneficial and good.

—The Dhammapada: The Self 7(163)

The idea of predestination is seen in the Old Testament where it is mentioned that we pay for the sins of the previous six generations. Astrology should lead us to the right approach towards our destinies. We must study our horoscopes until we discover our destinies, knowing that we are pushed by higher forces towards the fulfilment of them. Never give up hope. Learn how to preserve hope within oneself, as well as within others, by giving a good example.

Rejoice in your hope, be patient in tribulation, be constant in prayer.

—Romans 12:12

Everything has a purpose. Even books have their destinies (HABENT SUA FATA LIBELLI).

You can accept predestination, or you can fight it. You can use it for good or for evil. A strong person is one who suppresses whatever is bad. Through his own volition, he can change. A weak person is unable to fight destiny or to change it, but this weakness can be overcome. One must become his own helper by cultivating his will power through training.

For to everyone who has will more be given, and he will have abundance; but from him who has not, even what he has will be taken away.

—Matthew 25:29

If a child lacks will power, he should have help from his parents. The sensitivity of a person can change his destiny in that it may attune him to higher forces. We cannot change the nature of the planets. We can change, however, our own natures by improving the way we receive the planetary influences, but such a change may bring overcompensation. According to Epictetus (the Greek philosopher of the First Century A.D.), if anything depends solely on you, you may achieve it. Achievement is aided by an increase in the influences of Jupiter (protection) and a decrease in the influences of Saturn (fate/destiny).

As was said earlier, Saturn is the planet of destiny and fate, and it is also sometimes called the "Guardian of the Threshold." If you are highly evolved, you can escape much of Saturn's influences. It is possible for this to occur also in psychoanalysis, but this may prove very dangerous because by escaping, you remove simultaneously the threshold between the conscious and the unconscious.

Since you can change the way you receive planetary influences, the attitude of "I cannot change them" is an attitude of weakness. You are not the same person from birth to death. You change seven times during your life, because there are seven age groups, each ruled by a different planet. The sequence is as follows: Moon, Mercury, Venus, Sun, Mars, Jupiter, and Saturn.

And one man in his time plays many parts, His acts being seven ages.

> —*As You Like It*,
> William Shakespeare

Juventus ventus. (Youth is like the wind.)

> —Roman Proverb

Youths have exalted notions because they have not yet been humbled by life or learned its necessary limitations.

> —Aristotle

The search for the future is also the search for free will. In physics, free will does not exist. Free will in astrology is shown by how we modify planetary influences. A serious student of astrology knows that free will does exist, but to a limited extent. Free will is a gift from God; how much of it we have, we do not know.

Because you shut the Kingdom of Heaven against men; for you neither enter yourselves, nor allow those who enter to go in.

> —Matthew 23:15

In a horoscope, the Sun, through its placement and the sign it is in, will indicate how much free will there is. A well-aspected Sun in its own domicile and in an angular house, will provide the will power to counteract the bad influences of destiny. Free will cannot stop time or the day of death. The simpler the person, the less free will he has. The more evolved the person, the more free will he has.

I preferred to do nothing without your consent in order that your goodness might not be by compulsion but of your own free will.

—Philemon 14

There is a great problem whenever we study a birth chart in determining how much free will there is and how much destiny. An astrologer should not be permitted to go against the idea of free will; it would be unethical for him to negate free will.

Good and Bad Fortune

There are fortunate and unfortunate horoscopes. If you have a lucky horoscope, whatever you do will prove advantageous. Lucky people, as a rule, radiate positive vibrations. A person is lucky if he were born at a lucky hour, i.e., with a beneficial ascending sign. Usually, the ascendant of such a person is connected with the planet Jupiter and/or Venus.

Good fortune is having harmony and a good Moon, which will give the right instinctive drives. Good fortune starts with having a goal, but when you have a goal, you must realize it. Achievements bring strength.

One should become a philosopher, however, and realize that good luck contains misfortunes and bad luck contains fortunes (blessings in disguise). Whether a horoscope is good or bad depends also upon the quantity of the planetary influences. Too much or too little (the extremes) of an influence should be considered negative.

Good fortune depends also upon how you react to and receive the planetary influences. A smiling face tends to attract good luck. (You learn to smile with the influence of Venus.)

Lucky is the person whose radiations are good for the others, who radiates Jupiterian vibrations or who picks up the radiations of Jupiter. Generally, wherever you find Jupiter in a horoscope, you find good fortune.

The Sun in Cancer brings luck, since Jupiter rules the sign of Cancer through exaltation.

You are fortunate if you have a good Seventh House, the house of marriage and partners.

Why some people have good fortune and others bad fortune sometimes cannot be answered even from the horoscope, but if you have harmonious connections between the natal horoscope and the zodiac, generally, you are fortunate.

There are certain human beings who are protected and others who are destroyed, as if there were higher forces at work. These cases cannot be rationally explained. Lucky is the person who accepts his destiny.

Harmony versus Disharmony

Harmony creates happiness in the human being. The most important consideration is the way in which you receive the planetary influences and how far you can go in establishing harmony between the archetype (the zodiac) and your birth chart. As stated previously, you are fortunate if you have harmonious connections between your natal horoscope and the zodiac.

A person is ethical who is in harmony with the laws of nature and who has principles to which he sticks.

The less materialistic you are, the more you are in harmony with nature.

To achieve peace of mind, you must aim at taking the middle path (the center). Any deviation from the center is a deviation from harmony. Harmony cannot exist without motion. We need motion to continue the perpetual circle symbolized in ancient Greek mythology by the snake devouring its tail. To have harmony in oneself, one must apply the right thinking.

A good horoscope is the one that brings inner harmony. How much you are in harmony with another person depends in part upon how much you are in harmony with yourself; therefore, you must first learn to establish harmony in yourself, and then learn to live in harmony with others.

In order to be harmonious, a horoscope should have one of each of the signs in a triplicity on the cusps of houses 1, 5, and 9. For example, if Aries is on the ascendant, Leo should be on the Fifth House cusp and Sagittarius on the Ninth. What is good is harmonious. Harmony is the key to everything and has to be taken as a necessity. If you achieve harmony, you will be on the right track to fulfilling your destiny (your horoscope).

In order to interpret a horoscope, with the goal of helping the native to achieve harmony, it is important, among other considerations, to look, before judging, at the position in the horoscope of the archetypal rulers. In this way we are going from the particular (the native's birth chart) to the general (the Zodiac). If in a horoscope the harmony is disturbed, it cannot be considered a good horoscope. Disharmonious horoscopes need more fortitude in order to face the trials of life. You have to determine what causes the disharmony. Too much or too little means disharmony, and disharmony may cause a sickness.

Sickness is one of the enemies of concentration.

—Pantanjali, Book I:30

As long as you don't work against your health, you will not get sick. Health is achieved through harmony. One should be able to be his own physician. Our psychologies cause our sicknesses. The maintenance of a high level of intellectual performance, according to Dr. Warner Schaie, requires compliance with the use-it-or-lose-it principle. To slow the aging process, everyone should learn to influence his own hormones. The less earthbound you are, the more you are in harmony with nature. Look to things that are healthy and in the right quantity. Paracelsus, who went to Hungary in order to obtain crystals that had a great healing power, found that health is preserved with the same element when one is healthy, and healing is achieved from the opposite element when one is sick.

Quantity is more important than quality. In astrology, good and bad depends on quantity. A planet may or may not accentuate harmony, depending upon the quantity of its influence. Good reflects the right quantity. Bad reflects the wrong quantity (too much or too little). Extremes are bad. Any deviation from harmony represents a danger. You can establish harmony through the TAO, but it is very difficult for Westerners, who worship the Sun. The TAO is an Eastern philosophy, and Easterners worship the Moon.

Among others, Kepler (the astronomer and astrologer of the 16th century) sought the laws of harmony. To achieve harmony, one has to aim at a balance in oneself in the middle between extremes, where the quantity of the planetary influences is not excessive.

Any virtue reflects the middle road between two vices which encompass it as its two extremes. Extremes of prudence are wile and foolishness. Extremes of temperance are the fulfilment of the desires of the flesh and any kind of affliction an individual will impose upon himself. Extremes of magnanimity are pusillanimity and rashness. Justice has for extremes, cruelty and leniency.

—Georges Villefranche,
Astrologie Esotérique

One way in which to help to achieve harmony is to learn from the opposite. One's opposite sign helps with one's psychological problems as does, sometimes, the sign immediately following one's own. There are cases when disharmony can bring evolution and if a person is strong, disharmony is even advisable. The simpler a person is, the more he needs harmony.

According to the Kabbalah, the three enemies of man are the mouth, the stomach, and the sex organs.

> Guarding speech, controlling mind, not doing wrong with the body, a man keeps the three enemies to action clear and thus finds the path shown by the life.
>
> —The Dhammapada: The Path 9(281)

> Him I call a Brahamana who offends not by body, speech or mind; who is controlled in these three things.
>
> —The Dhammapada: The Brahamana 9(391)

> For anyone who eats and drinks without discerning the body, eats and drinks judgment upon himself. That is why many of you are weak and ill, and some have died.
>
> —1 Corinthians 11:29,30

> Hear and understand; not what goes into the mouth defiles a man, but what comes out of the mouth, this defiles a man.
>
> —Matthew 15:11

> But what comes of the mouth proceeds from the heart, and this defiles a man. For out of the heart come evil thoughts, murder, adultery, fornication, theft, false witness, slander. These are what defiles a man; but to eat with unwashed hands does not defile a man.
>
> —Matthew 15:18–20

> Well controlled, indeed are the wise; they have mastery over body, tongue and mind.
>
> —The Dhammapada: Anger 14(234)

The sky (the Zodiac) is always in harmony and in peace.

Only a few escape into the heavenly light.

—The Dhammapada: The World 8(174)

Blessed are the pure in heart, for they shall see God.

—Matthew 5:8

Time

Everything in nature has a given lifespan. One cannot fight time. An astrologer must solve the problem of time, i.e., how to integrate it. To understand one's destiny, and to fulfill it, is the solution to the problem of time. A simple person does not know time; a more evolved person knows time; a good astrologer can see what lies ahead, but he must be careful that this knowledge is used properly, and with great foresight, since foreknowledge does not necessarily produce happiness. What is most important in astrology is the future, since the present becomes the past.

> Forget the former things; do not dwell on the past.
>
> —Isaiah 43:18

The future has to do with the Tenth House (the house of realization and of destiny). People nowadays are concerned only with the present. They neglect thinking about the future, for which has been predicted geophysical catastrophies. Today, the times make it difficult for a happy approach to life. All living creatures undergo changes caused by the rhythms of nature. When you complicate something, for example, by introducing the concept of time, you deepen it. Primitive people do not use the concept of time.

King Solomon must have taken time as an expression of wisdom. The Seal of Solomon, a symbol of wisdom, which can also be interpreted as a symbol of time, is a six-pointed star formed of two interlocking equilateral triangles. In the archetype, the cusps of the Tenth, the Second and the Sixth Houses form one equilateral triangle (the upper triangle of the seal), which corresponds to the triplicity indicating the future. The other equilateral triangle (the lower triangle), formed by joining the cusps of the Fourth, the Eighth, and the Twelfth Houses, corresponds to the triplicity representing the past and the present.

The right time for things is not governed by the horoscope. The wisdom in the morning is different from that in the afternoon or in the evening.

To the biologist, time and space are things of immediate concern, with time being the most important element. Time and space are not equal. Space shows no wisdom. The space element in a horoscope is shown by the horizon, i.e., the line linking the cusp of the First and Seventh Houses (the ascendant and the descendant). It is not reflected in the Seal of Solomon, because King Solomon did not consider time and space to be equal.

One can alter the space element by changing one's location. A person is influenced by his environment, but he can also influence the environment, as in the case of a good teacher having a beneficial impact on his students. Education and environment are very important. The study of astrology must take into consideration not only the time of birth, but also the environment.

Since he cannot fight time, the wise man will never go against it. Saturn is the planet connected with time. So, the search of Saturn is for time. Foresight is related to the time element, and survival, of primary importance in life, is based on foresight. Intelligence is based on foresight. In fact, our whole lives are based on foresight, but since foresight is connected with Saturn and the Moon, it may bring anxiety.

Intelligence enables one to see what is worth seeing, i.e., what is substantial, relevant, and desirable. Sophistication is foresight. Statesmen must have it.

Nowadays, time is connected with the Tenth House (destiny, realization, profession) and the Fourth House (home, environment). The Tenth and Fourth Houses are the only houses between which you need cooperation (one's profession and one's home or parents). It is said at wedding celebrations in the Greek Orthodox Church, "The blessings of parents sustain the foundations of a home." The line linking the cusps of the Tenth and Fourth Houses in a horoscope corresponds to the time element. It is perpendicular to the horizon and forms a cross with it by dividing the horizon in two equal parts.

When studying a horoscope, the first question one should ask is what events will take place, the second is when will they take place, and the third is how to escape bad events.

It is very important to get rid of wrong thinking and obstructive tendencies. Wrong thinking occurs when one element is missing, and this is often the time element.

For good judgement, an astrologer needs a good Moon (the unconscious) and a good Saturn, since he searches for the future.

In order to make a prediction in a solar or lunar chart, one must always look for a repetition of that which is in the natal chart, in terms of the aspects and the planets involved. In a general way, a repetition is very important. It may be in the zodiac (the archetype), in the houses (the natal place), or in both. A solar or lunar return chart must always be compared to the natal horoscope and never be studied alone. If, in a solar return, the influence of the planets, by their positions, is disadvantageous, their influence can be decreased if the solar return is calculated for a different longitude and latitude.

As was said previously, whoever looks to the future must focus on how to escape bad events. The future is here, the future is now. It is possible to foresee future events and trends, but if you foresee them and predict them to your enquirer, you risk taking away his or her free will.

In directional astrology, we transform space into time and time into space.

Each year the Sun moves 59 minutes 8 seconds around the horoscope. One must consider the speed of the Sun at birth.

For predictive astrology consider, in the following order:

1) ***The natal horoscope***.

2) ***The primary directions***. These are most accurate when one knows the exact birth time. If the exact time of birth is unknown to the native, it can be determined by the astrologer through the examination of the dates of important events in the life of the native. Bad aspects to the progressed mid-heaven signify setbacks in the profession and bad aspects to the progressed ascendant reflect sicknesses.

3) ***The solar revolution***. The solar revolution is to be judged only in conjunction with the natal horoscope.

4) ***The lunar revolution***. The lunar revolution is to be judged only in conjunction with the natal horoscope.

5) ***The transits***. Any transit that repeats an aspect found in the natal horoscope will have a greater impact than one that does not. There will also be a greater impact on the native each time a transiting planet passes over a place where a natal planet is either posited or sends an aspect. With transits, one must consider the following:
   a) the nature of the transiting planet.
   b) the aspects that the transiting planet forms.
   c) the house in which it transits.
   d) the zodiacal state of the transiting planet.

As to planets in aspect:

1) benefic planets in good aspect with one another are big helpers. A
   truly good aspect is that between two beneficial planets.
2) benefic planets in bad aspect are small destroyers.
3) malefic planets in bad aspect are big destroyers.
4) malefic planets in good aspect are small helpers.

In order to escape bad events, one has to act against bad forthcoming planetary influences (and the anxiety they produce) with the right thinking.

Vigilantibus non dormientibus urgentis sic veniunt. (To the vigilants and not to those that sleep the deeds bring results.)

—Julius Caesar

Each person should prepare his answer before the question is asked.

It is difficult to sense the right time to make a decision, but some decision is better than no decision at all. It is better to fail than not to struggle. Indecision is, above all else, worse than a bad choice. Generally, one should neither hang on nor postpone his action. One should never judge that it is too soon or too late for something. Only at the end of one's life will he be able to tell whether he acted too soon or too late.

George Orwell once said, "Who controls the past, controls the future and who controls the present controls the past."

For everything there is a season, and a time
for every matter under heaven:
a time to be born, and a time to die;
a time to plant and a time to pluck up what is planted;
a time to kill and a time to heal;
a time to break down and a time to build up;
a time to weep and a time to laugh;
a time to mourn and a time to dance;
a time to cast away stones and
a time to gather stones together;
a time to embrace and a time to refrain from embracing;
a time to seek and a time to lose;
a time to keep and a time to chase away:
a time to reap and a time to sow;
a time to keep silence and a time to speak;
a time to love and a time to hate;
a time for war and a time for peace.

—Ecclesiastes 3:1–15

Wisdom

By endeavour, by vigilance, by discipline and self-control, let the wise man make for himself an island which no flood can overwhelm.

—The Dhammapada: Vigilance 5(25)

Happy is the man who finds wisdom and the man who gets understanding.

—Proverbs 3:13

The desire for wisdom is the highest desire for a human being to have. Moderation is the key to wisdom, which is achieved through will power and patience. Wisdom is never practical. It can be acquired through astrology, since through astrology one learns that everything has a purpose. A wise man is in harmony with the laws of nature.

Sagittarius is the sign of wisdom. The house of wisdom or higher knowledge is the Ninth. It is often called the House of God. Jupiter, the protector, is the ruler of the Ninth House, which corresponds to the sign of Sagittarius. Jupiter represents the higher values of wisdom, which bring inner peace. Jupiter is the opposite of Mercury, the ruler of the Third House, which corresponds to the sign of Gemini. That is why a good aspect between Mercury and Jupiter is not necessarily beneficial.

"ΦΡΟΝΗΣΙΣ," i.e., Phronesis:

Practical wisdom, that by mixing reason, good sense, and experience, guides all moral life and action.

—Aristotle

The price of wisdom is suffering. To suffer means to sustain changes. One must get rid of the resistance to change. Awareness is the key to change. The Ninth House in the archetype is the Tenth House (house of destiny and realization) of the Twelfth House of the archetype (house of suffering).

The sign of Cancer (Fourth House in the archetype) is also a sign of wisdom, since Jupiter is exalted there. The Fourth House in the ar-

14

chetype is the Eighth House (house of regeneration) of Sagittarius (the Ninth House). Thus, wisdom (higher knowledge) manifests itself when you come to exaltation. Exaltation goes for purity. Wisdom is connected with water and fire, and intelligence with air and earth. This is because Jupiter is connected with water and fire signs and Mercury with air and earth signs. Intelligence is obtained through analysis, through details. Wisdom is obtained through synthesis. Wisdom sees both sides. Life is synthesis. Intelligence will realize itself in wisdom.

> Then I will give you shepherds after my own heart who will lead you with knowledge and understanding.
>
> —Jeremiah 3:15

The Third house, which is the house of the mind, corresponding to the sign of Gemini in the Zodiac, provides the foundation for much of one's daily life.

> To watch the mind is conducive to happiness. The tame mind is the bearer of happiness.
>
> —The Dhammapada: Mind 4 and 3 (36) and (35)

The simple person will put the blame on others.

> Easy it is to see the faults of the others: difficult it is to see our own.
>
> —The Dhammapada: Impurity 18(252)

An intelligent person blames himself. The wise man blames nobody.

> He is a real pundit who is tranquil, free from hatred, free from fear.
>
> —The Dhammapada: One Established in the Law 3(258)

The planets decrease our freedom. The ideal for men would be to be completely free of planetary influences.

> Riches destroy the foolish, not those who seek the beyond. By his craving for possessions the foolish man destroys himself.
>
> —The Dhammapada: Craving 22(355)

Forgive me if my desire was sin. I dreamed to have reared and nurtured thee to the divinest destinies my visions could foresee. Betimes as the mortal part was strengthened against disease to have purified the spiritual from every sin; to have led thee, heaven upon heaven, through the holy ecstasies which make up the existence of the orders that dwell on high; to have formed, from thy sublime affections, the pure and ever-living communication between thy mother and myself. The dream was but a dream—it is no more! In sight myself of the grave, I feel at last through the portals of the grave lies the true initiation into the holy and the wise. Beyond those portals I await ye both, beloved pilgrims!

> —*Zanoni*
> E. Bulwer Lytton

Wisdom is also connected with the Moon (the unconscious). The emotions are completely dependent on the unconscious. While, according to Dr. Seymour Epstein, the emotions are not connected with intelligence, the intellectual ability of people determines how effectively they can manage their emotions.

Love is wisdom, but you cannot struggle to have love or to give love to another person.

Love does not insist on its own way; it is not irritable or resentful.

> —1 Corinthians 13:5

Wisdom is love. A person who loves and smiles is not afraid of life. The older you get, the more you should concentrate on wisdom.

For I myself find that as age blunts one's enjoyment of physical pleasures, one's desire for rational conversation, and one's enjoyment of it, increases correspondingly.

> —Plato's *Republic*, 328d

For if men are sensible and good tempered, old age is easy enough to bear; if not, youth as well as age is a burden.

> —Plato's *Republic* 329d.

The acquiring of wisdom is accelerated when one gets rid of anxiety, anxiety often being an exaggerated desire for self-preservation.

To know your own nature is the key to wisdom.

How far can you go, if you do not know yourself?

> —Hillel

The advice of the French is to change one's nature (*"Changer la nature"*). The advice of the Germans is to follow necessity and not your own nature.

The building of one's profession (the Tenth House) will bring marriage (the Seventh House), which in turn will bring a home (the Fourth House). A good profession is the best solution for happiness.

Wisdom is optimism, freedom, and foresight. The wise man does not worry. The amount of wisdom one has will depend on the degree one has learned to integrate time.

In order to become wise in our "civilized" society, one needs money, and one must work for other people.

One must try to understand and to fulfill one's own horoscope, in order to attain wisdom.

As a person becomes wiser, he evolves from the Moon to Mercury, from Mercury to Venus, from Venus to the Sun, from the Sun to Mars, from Mars to Jupiter and from Jupiter to Saturn. That is why the most important planet is the planet of one's age group; it will determine how, at a particular age, one will receive the planetary influences.

According to the Kabbalah (oral tradition), wisdom should not be written down. It has been said that

Those who know do not speak; those who speak do not know.

—TAO TE KING: *Paradoxes*

Wisdom can be communicated verbally, but not necessarily understood by others.

Truly, I say to you, many prophets and righteous men longed to see what you see, and did not see it, and to hear what you hear, and did not hear it.

—Matthew 13:17

Wisdom can be communicated through initiation.

And Melchizedek King of Salem brought out bread and wine; he was priest of God Most High. And he blessed him and said, "Blessed be Abram by God Most High, maker of heaven and earth, and blessed be God Most High, who has delivered your enemies into your hands!"

—Genesis 15:18–20

And the Lord said to him, "Go, return on your way to the wilderness of Damascus: and when you arrive you shall anoint Hazael . . . and Elijah the son of Sophet of Abel—Meholah you should anoint to be prophet in your place . . . I . . . Elijah passed by him and cast his mantle upon him."

—Kings I, 19:15,16,19

A wise man without a good Mercury will not be able to communicate. (Mercury, being the ruler of Gemini, the first sign of the airy triplicity in the Zodiac, represents intelligence and communication.)

The mind of the wise makes his speech judicious and adds persuasiveness to his lips.

—Proverbs 16:23

The wise of heart is called a man of discernment and pleasant speech increases persuasiveness.

—Proverbs 16:21

A wise man works to increase the beneficial influence of his Jupiter.

The memory of the righteous is a blessing, but the name of the wicked will not.

—Proverbs 10:7

Values

Whenever you examine a horoscope, you should determine the values therein (which depend upon the zodiacal state of the planets) and see whether they are conscious or unconscious, and whether the will can realize them.

Each person can find his mission in life by examining his horoscope. First, look at the ascendant; second, look at the Moon; third, look at the Sun. The horoscope guides us in completing the tasks that we have to fulfill on earth. We can tell if somebody is evolved by his values. We each form our own values, and our values change as we get older. The values of a person will depend partly upon his age group.

One must believe in predestination and in free will. Predestination can be changed. We may make life better or worse for ourselves by changing our ideas, our values, and our environments. A way must be found for the will to work on all levels, thus opening the path to a higher perception of the meaning of life. With self-improvement you can develop the possibility for change. Higher values bring us inner peace—harmony in ourselves. The problem often becomes how to preserve our higher values.

Each planet is connected with a ductless gland. Mercury especially is connected with the thyroid gland, Neptune with the pineal gland, and Uranus with the parathyroid glands.

A good and wise man (ΑΝΗΡ ΚΑΛΟΣ ΚΑΓΑΘΟΣ) must be in harmony with the laws of nature and must have harmony in himself. He will then be able to influence the functions of his ductless glands, which regulate aging and psychology. The process of aging or decay occurs when cell reproduction comes to an end or slows down. You can regulate the aging process if you manage to become less concerned with earthly values.

Upgrading yourself without losing your ethics is very difficult, since you generally upgrade yourself at the expense of others.

Today, all the people of the earth undergo a lowering of values. In fact, nowadays many people don't have values at all, or only very low ones. We are living in a civilization where aggressiveness seems to be necessary. The majority of people seek physical values (pleasure and material gain) and the higher (spiritual) values have nearly disappeared.

> Him I call a Brahamana who is friendly among the hostiles, mild among
> the violent, ungrasping among the greedy.

> —The Dhammapada: The Brahamana 21(406)

A spiritually oriented individual is one whose values with regard to time and space are excellent.

A person with bad values is attracted to earthly life, to the material. What makes our values right or wrong? Our values are right if they give better health, and advancement without harming the others. Our values are wrong if ourselves or others are harmed. No one is forced to have the right values.

When studying the values of a person from his horoscope, one should consider the native's family and his genes, since each family has different values. As a rule, children are conditioned to represent the values of the father.

> If any one does not provide for his relatives, and especially for his own
> family, he has disowned his faith and is worse than an unbeliever.

> —2 Timothy 5:8

The desire for the realization of one's instincts is one of the right values for a human being to have.

The Sun should serve to realize the instincts in a civilized way. The two enemies of good values are too much of something or too little of something. The key to everything is moderation. If you are spiritually evolved, you will never go to extremes.

An exalted planet gives high (spiritual) values. Spiritual values enable one to work for suffering people. Generally speaking, planets in a good zodiacal state will bring spiritual values.

The difference between similar horoscopes is found in the values they represent. A person whose values are wrong is dangerous. Values depend partly on the judgement of a person and partly on his age group. For the right judgement and thinking, one needs a good analytical mind (Mercury), a good ability to synthesize (Jupiter), and a good unconscious (Moon).

In order to be happy, you must have a good Fourth House and a good Twelfth House. The Fourth House is very important in childhood. Happiness must start in the family. The Fourth House represents not only the beginning of life, but also the end of it. The Fourth House also indicates the genes, the parental values, the family background, and the community. It is best to be born with healthy genes.

If the ruler of the Twelfth House is in fall, you will lack the right values, and will not be inclined to fight for yourself. Thus, you will lack independence.

One has to fight against destructive planetary influences (which can cause physical, mental, and emotional problems) in order to maintain one's values, sanity, and self-respect.

Ignorance, egoism, desire, and aversion are considered to be afflictions that lead to emotional problems.

Afflictions are to be got rid of by meditation.

—Patanjali, Book II:11

A man of quick temper acts foolishly, but a man of discretion is patient.

—Proverbs 14:17

There is no fire like passion;
there is no strangler like hate;
there is no net like delusion;
there is no torrent like craving.

—The Dhammapada: Impurity 17(251)

Almost everything depends on the receiver. It may be said that the masochist searches for the sadist, and the victim looks for the murderer. What is important is not the person who preaches, but the people who listen.

Habits are second nature. If you seek new values, you must create new habits.

In the Western world, helping other people by giving a good example is important. In India, you have only to fulfill your karma. Hence, there is a difference in values between the West and the East. The highest values are symbolized by the planet Jupiter.

Overcompensation

People may master their shortcomings after discovering what is missing in their horoscopes. Each of us has the need to make his horoscope complete, and we may overcompensate in order to achieve this.

When the ruler of the ascendant is in detriment or in fall, it can cause psychological problems such as a poor self-image. We can work against this only by changing our environments and/or by changing our values through overcompensation. Overcompensation will usually occur if the ruler of the ascendant, while being in detriment or in fall, is in an angular house.

To the question, "Can we fight against our horoscopes?," the answer is that it is always difficult to go against our horoscopes. You have to accept limitations. A wise man will take limitation as a blessing and will not expect miracles.

You cannot change the nature of a planet. You can change only the way you receive the planet's influence, i.e., its quantity. When you change the planet's quantity, you will change your nature. This may, in turn, as said previously, cause you to overcompensate.

Whoever loves discipline loves knowledge, but he who hates reproof is stupid.

—Proverbs 12:1

When the ruler of the Twelfth House is in fall, a person will not have the right values and won't fight. He should learn to fight by overcompensation via the opposite sign on the cusp of the opposite house (in this example, the Sixth House, the house of work, health, and service), and to be completely independent of what others do and say.

The spirit of man is the lamp of the Lord, searching all his innermost parts.

—Proverbs 20:27

When the ruler of the horoscope is in detriment, one should study its dispositor, and then the final dispositor.

Overcompensation may occur in highly spiritually evolved individuals who do not conform to the expectations of their horoscopes, and who take the disharmonious aspects of their birth charts as drives for evolution. Disharmony is desirable in such cases.

Anxiety can be a cause of overcompensation. Anxiety is caused by the horoscope itself, and also by the values learned in the home, i.e., the upbringing. Therefore, it is very important for a child not to be brought up with the wrong social values.

Opposite signs work together through cooperation. Each sign must learn from its opposite sign, which acts as its partner. You learn from the opposite sign how to adjust to reality. Rudolf Steiner (the founder of Anthroposophy) changed the negative qualities of his Scorpio ascendant by becoming a metaphysician. The sign of Scorpio has the power within it to direct its desires to a higher purpose. (Steiner, however, overcompensated to such an extent that he went to the extreme.)

With regard to changing one's nature by overcompensation, it is unknown just how far the deepest nature of an individual can change. Perhaps it is indicated by the position of Pluto in the horoscope, and the aspects Pluto sends. Pluto has to do with the impact and the pressure of the unconscious on the conscious.

Aleister Crowley's horoscope shows overcompensation. With no aspect between his Sun in Libra and his Moon in Pisces, there is no connection between the conscious and the unconscious.

From the practical point of view, it is preferable for a horoscope not to show extremes, neither by nature nor by overcompensation.

How can one challenge one's nature without overcompensating? Can one actually change one's nature? No psychiatrist has ever managed to change the nature of his patient completely, but one can try by:

1) Avoiding extremes and all exaggeration.

2) Learning from the sign opposite one's rising sign.

3) Not fighting with others.

All those who desire a spiritual approach must have a strong Neptune. As to the question: "Is the spiritual approach to be found in the Ninth House of the Archetype (Sagittarius) or the Eighth House (Scorpio)?," it has been said, "When the snake burns away, the Phoenix comes out." Everyone has to burn his own snake first; that is, in order to dedicate himself to higher knowledge, one must first control his desires, or, put another way, go from the Eighth House to the Ninth.

What has more value for the spiritual approach, a person born with exalted planets, or a person with planets in fall or detriment, who overcompensates? In the Orient, planets in exaltation are preferred for the true metaphysical approach, but in the West, overcompensation is preferred. To the Westerner, exaltation equals neurosis.

With planets in exaltation, a person has a sense of a higher mission, which reflects his very high metaphysical values.

> Because we look not to the things that are seen but to the things that are unseen; for the things that are unseen are eternal.

> —2 Corinthians 4:18

Exalted planets can create difficulties for an individual in his daily life, so that he will have to work a lot to adjust himself.

Evolution

Astrology is the best tool for understanding the problems of life and for helping us to evolve. In order to evolve, we must attempt to learn why we are here. The more one evolves, the more responsible he becomes. The only purpose of astrology is to understand our own evolutions, including that of the unconscious. The key to our cravings is in our horoscopes. Complete spiritual evolution is impossible owing to the limits of the body, the soul, and the mind. We can come close to knowing reality only if we evolve, but even if we evolve, we still won't know reality.

For many things are shown to thee above the understanding of men.

—Ecclesiasticus II:25

When you get rid of anxiety, your evolution is put on the right path.

There is no place higher than tranquility.

—The Dhammapada: Happiness 6(202)

According to Theosophists, the highest degree of evolution can be achieved through great suffering, but then you must believe in KARMA. The key to evolution is to consider the time element.

The integration of time and patience are signs of evolution. Time can make a person become evolved, and an evolved individual will no longer fear that time will not help him in achieving his goals. He will heed the familiar saying "Haste means waste."

For the most High is the patient rewarder.

—Ecclesiasticus V:4

How much can one evolve, and how far can he adjust himself to the time element? It will depend partly on his degree of patience. Patience requires a sustained attention and increases intelligence and memory.

Attention is fixing the mind on a place, object or subject.

—Patanjali, Book III:1

In attempting to determine the purpose of life, one has to decide if there is spiritual evolution, or if everything is evolution on the material plane. Spiritual evolution can be achieved by learning more about the secrets of life and death. Spiritual evolution requires one to learn how to perceive the world differently, i.e., no longer on the material plane.

And there, in the very cell beside her own, the atheist, Nicot, sits stolid amidst the darkness, and hugs the thought of Danton, that death is nothingness . . . Still staring into space, gnawing his livid lip, he lopped upon the darkness, convinced that darkness is for ever and for ever!

—Zanoni
Sir Edward Bulwer Lytton

We have to be tremendously evolved not to be afraid of death.

Sons are no protection, nor father, nor kinsmen, when one is seized by death. There is no help from relations when death seizes one.

—The Dhammapada: The Path 16(288)

"To be free from the fear of death does not mean pretending to oneself, in one's good hours, that one will not tremble in the face of death, and that there is nothing to fear. Rather, he who masters both life and death is free from fear of any kind to the extent that he is no longer capable of experiencing what fear feels like."

"Years of unceasing meditation have taught him (every master who practices an art moulded by Zen) that life and death are at bottom the same and belong to the same stratum of fact. He no longer knows what fear of life and terror of death are. He lives—and this is thoroughly characteristic of Zen—happily enough in the world but ready at any time to quit it without being in the least disturbed by the thought of death."

—Zen in the Art of Archery
Eugene Herrigel

For spiritual evolution, you have to go away from the earth, towards heaven. Evolved people acknowledge the existence of higher forces which guide us in fulfilling our tasks on earth. Our five senses are not sufficient. We never consider higher forces unless the planet Neptune

26

(representing the seventh sense) is strong in our horoscopes. A powerful Neptune enables one to see beyond the physical plane. It promotes inspiration and aspiration. Human beings are not yet evolved enough to understand higher forces completely. In the present stage of our evolution, our knowledge is insufficient. Life is full of secrets and does not give enough explanations.

The mistake of most human beings is that they rely only on their five senses and don't want to recognize higher forces. They forget that we are in the process of evolution.

It is up to each individual, according to the degree of his own evolution, to discover, attract, and attune himself to these higher forces in the right way in order to find his mission and fulfill his destiny. Nonetheless, evolution cannot be taken as a profession and should not necessarily be accelerated.

The more evolved you are, the more you emanate radiations, and the more you receive very subtle vibrations.

Exaltation is connected with evolution. Truly spiritually evolved people may have several planets in exaltation, which, however, is not advantageous for daily earthly affairs, because exaltation does not give enough realism. Evolution increases the values of the conscious and brings increased freedom, but if you want to evolve, you need the will to do so. Evolution is achieved through sustained inspiration and an unfailing will power. Your will is your survival. In order to evolve, we can, and must, go against the negative tendencies in our horoscopes, by changing our values and our environments. We have to be dedicated in life. In order to survive, we have to follow necessity, not our natures. Evolution means evolving towards freedom.

If you continue in my word, you are truly my disciples, and you will know the truth, and the truth will make you free.

—John 8:31–32

For an evolved person, only the rising sign cannot be changed. Everything else in one's horoscope can be modified. Disharmony is more important for an evolved person because it produces a drive. The more simple you are, the more harmony you need.

To determine from a horoscope the degree of a person's evolution, you must combine the houses, the signs, the planets, and the aspects between the planets.

As stated previously, astrology is a guide to fulfilling our tasks on earth and in helping us to understand our evolution, which involves realizing our unconscious needs in a civilized way.

The forces of the soul (the Moon) must cooperate with those of the spirit (the Sun) in order for spiritual evolution to be attained.

The way you receive the planetary influences equals the degree of your evolution. If you undergo psychogenic training, you can change the way you receive the influences. Psychogenic training (Oriental Philosophy, breathing, and rotation of the heart chakra) will relieve you from anxiety.

> Thus it is written, "The first man Adam became a living being"; the last Adam became a life-giving spirit. But it is not the spiritual which is first but the physical, and then the spiritual.
>
> —1 Corinthians 15:45–46

The meaning of spirituality is evolution. Evolution will depend on how we receive and accept our destinies. The person who accepts his destiny is lucky. By studying our own horoscopes, we can better understand the influence of the higher forces that we receive. Astrology helps us to sense why we are here and how we can obtain an evolution.

For the Westerner, it is more difficult to "see" the invisible. In the West, the person with an evolved horoscope will not limit himself to his own evolution, but he will try to improve his environment. There will be an urge to go beyond the limits. In India, one has only to fulfill his own karma. There, a human being who is evolved takes limitation as a blessing and does not expect miracles.

Evolution can only be achieved through experience and trials resulting from relationship with others.

> Health is the greatest of gifts; contentment is the greatest wealth; trust is the best of relationships.
>
> —The Dhammapada: Happiness 15(204)

We pass through a lot of experiences with a lot of other human souls. You cannot evolve unless you work for other people. You will have, at the beginning, to work with other people in order to get experience. Thus, evolution will be indicated by one's Seventh House, the house of partnerships, and of other people in general.

And if the soul is to know itself, it must look into a soul.

—Plato (Alcibiades, 133B)

Life is very hard, and to be able to evolve, you have to fight.

The will (the Sun), which does not know mercy, is indispensable, if you want to evolve and to survive.

To realize the good, you need a tremendous spiritual evolution since "The many of this world are ill-natured" (The Dhammapada: The Elephant 1[320].

For the true spiritual approach, one has to take the middle path, which encompasses everything. "Never push too hard at the beginning." Too hard means too much. The key to everything is moderation. A good man must have harmony in himself. The spiritual approach is in harmony with the laws of nature.

> Extreme straightness is as bad as crookedness.
> Extreme cleverness is as bad as folly.
> Extreme fluency is as bad as stammering.

—TAO TE KING: Paradoxes

An evolved individual has the characteristic attitude of Pisces, which is "Love thy neighbour as thyself."

> Despise not the hungry soul;
> and provoke not the poor in his want.
> Afflict not the heart of the needy;
> and defer not to give to him that is in distress.

—Ecclesiasticus IV: 2,3

The more evolved you are, the more you are responsible for your actions. The less evolved you are, the less you are responsible for your actions, and the more you blame the planets.

The fault, dear Brutus, is not in the stars, but in ourselves.

—Julius Caesar
Shakespeare

As it has been stated previously, an astrologer must study the zodiac, namely the archetype (the archetype being more important for the evolved person than his own birth chart), and he must know how to decipher it, by going from the general to the particular, and from the particular to the general.

The more evolved one is, the more important the zodiac becomes, and the less important the natal horoscope. However, it is fortunate to have harmonious connections between the natal horoscope and the zodiac. In order to be happy, you must have a good Fourth House and a good Twelfth House.

The Fourth House is the most important house in a horoscope, since in the archetype it is the house ruled by the Moon (the unconscious). It is the house of the beginning and the end of the present incarnation. For that reason, when examining a horoscope, one should, after looking at the ascendant, look at the Moon, the natural ruler of the Fourth House in the zodiac.

In order to have a good Twelfth House, which must be excellent to pursue spiritual evolution, one must have a good Eleventh House. The gain of the Eleventh is in its Second House, i.e., the Twelfth.

The Twelfth House is the house of sufferings and of sicknesses that seem incurable. A good Third House will prevent Twelfth House sufferings, since one will develop the right approach through a sound judgement.

The Ascendant

The cusp of the First House is called the ascendant. The human being is represented by his or her ascendant.

The orb of the ascendant is 8 degrees 30 minutes.

The ascendant is the first consideration when interpreting a horoscope; it is the most important element and as a rule cannot be altered during the course of one's life. As to the question of changing the ascendant through will power, the answer is that in some cases this is possible through overcompensation; such was the case of Rudolf Steiner, who changed his Scorpio ascendant to a Libra one. However, since astrology is a science of observation, the matter of developing one's will within the context of a specific horoscope may well go beyond astrology.

The ascendant receives influences from the planets, and so is called a "receiver." It is not a "sender," because it does not send aspects the way in which the planets do. However, one could say that it gives off radiations. A person usually senses whether his own ascendant is in harmony with the ascendant of another person through these radiations. The ascendant shows how one will receive the planetary influences.

Happiness comes from having a good ascendant. The happy person receives the planetary influences differently from the unhappy one. One's ascendant is determined by one's time of birth. The true moment of birth of a child occurs with its first intake of air, or its first cry. According to the Kabbalists, a child cries because he knows he has to reincarnate.

The ascendant is the significator of life. It represents the physical and mental constitution (personality) of the native, the mental constitution being the most important. However, the ascendant must not be studied without the two other signs of its triplicity.

The ascendant represents the earth. One's drive should go from his ascendant to the Tenth House (the house of destiny). (The Tenth House also represents the parent of the opposite sex from that of the native.)

In the case of fanatics, who are driven by other people who give off strong radiations, the ascendant becomes unimportant, to the profit of the Seventh House (people one associates with).

The ascendant is four times more important than its ruler.
Four points are important to consider:

1) ***The ascendant.*** The more planets connected with the ascendant
and the mid-heaven, the greater the power drive will be. As a
general rule, an earthy sign on the ascendant is not desirable,
because earth takes away one's freedom. If, in a horoscope, there
are four or more planets in a sign, that sign will compete with the
rising sign in influence. Four or more planets in a sign is called a
stellium.

2) ***The aspects received by the ascendant.***

3) ***The ruler of the ascendant.*** If the ruler of the ascendant is not in
honour of triplicity, other signs in the chart may assume greater
importance than the sign on the ascendant. When the ruler of the
ascendant is in detriment or in fall, one should look at the ruler's
dispositor, and then at its final dispositor. Whenever the ruler of the
ascendant is in the Tenth House, the native will take his future into
his own hands, because there will be a strong drive towards the
realization of his profession. When the ruler of the ascendant is in
the Twelfth House, the native may feel imprisoned. However, it is
important to look at the position in the horoscope of the archetypal
rulers of the Twelfth House (Jupiter and Neptune), among other
considerations, before judging. In this way, we are going from the
particular (the native's Twelfth House) to the general (the archetypal Twelfth House). If the ruler of the ascendant is in detriment in the Twelfth House, the native will have an inferiority
complex and a given shyness. In general, whenever the ruler of the
ascendant is in fall or in detriment, there will be an inferiority
complex, and it will be necessary to overcompensate in order to
overcome the given weakness. It is also considered undesirable for
the ruler of the ascendant to be the lowest planet in a birth chart,
i.e., the one closest to the i.c. (imum coeli), the Fourth House cusp.

4) ***Aspects received by the ruler of the ascendant.*** We examine
these aspects in two ways:
   a) from the sky to the earth, e.g., Venus, ruler of the ascendant,
      posited in Gemini, First House, will receive trines from
      Aquarius and Libra and squares from Virgo and Pisces.
   b) from the earth to the sky, e.g., Venus, ruler of the ascendant,

will receive trines from the Fifth and the Ninth houses and squares from the Fourth and the Tenth houses.

The houses of the horoscope are around the earth. The signs of the Zodiac are in the sky. The horoscope is a combination of the sky (the signs) and the earth (the houses).

Through the degrees at which the planets are positioned, we can determine the strength of the aspects, hence the quantity of the influences. The power of the rising sign is twice that of the Moon and four times that of the Sun.

It is easier to overcome difficulties with a male ascendant because the conscious (will power) is stronger, while with a female ascendant, the unconscious (instinct) is stronger.

One's self-image is connected with the ruler of the ascendant. If the ruler of the ascendant is in an angular house (1,4,7,10), there will be a strong drive. If it is in the Sixth House, there will be a lack of drive, because between the ascendant and the Sixth House, there is no aspect. The Sixth House is not considered to be a good house, because it is the house of short sicknesses, work, and servitude.

The happiness or unhappiness of children depends to a great extent on their parents and their environment. A child needs a good father, as well as a happy mother. A good horoscope is the one that indicates good parents.

Hear, my son, your father's instruction, and reject not your mother's teaching; for they are a fair garland for your head, and pendants for your neck.

—Proverbs 1:8,9

The Lights

Neither the Sun nor the Moon are planets. The Sun and the Moon are called the two lights. They should cooperate. There should be an equilibrium between the will of the Sun and the instincts of the Moon, with the Sun realizing the unconscious needs of the Moon. Thus, the Moon must be directed by the Sun, or, said in another way, the instincts must be directed by the will in a civilized fashion.

In a horoscope, the Kingdom of the Sun is above the horizon, and the Kingdom of the Moon is below the horizon. The Sun is electric and is connected with the grey cells of the brain, while the Moon is magnetic and is connected with the feminine cells of the brain.

> There are celestial bodies and there are terrestrial bodies: but the glory of the celestial body is one, and the glory of the terrestrial is another. There is one glory of the Sun and another glory of the Moon, and another glory of the stars; for star differs from star in glory.
>
> —1 Corinthians 15:40–41

☉ THE SUN

The Moon and the Earth receive influences. The Sun serves to realize the Moon, or, to put it another way, the day serves to realize the night. The night is often dangerous.

> For you are all sons of light and sons of the day: we are not of the night or of darkness.
>
> —1 Thessalonians 5:5

The Sun directs the instincts, but it does not guarantee that the instincts will manifest themselves in a civilized way. This will depend on the aspects in the birth chart under examination, as well as the zodiacal states of the Moon and of the Sun.

The Sun, the strongest of the heavenly bodies in a horoscope, is warm and dry. It is a sender of influences. Its orb is 17 degrees.

The Sun never appears retrograde.

The Sun represents the father, the will, and the consciousness or spirit. It is connected with light, vitality, independence, organization, and government. One's will can be increased through training. A person is under the influence of the Sun from the age of twenty-one to forty-two.

The Sun does not know fear or anxiety. In fact, the Sun can help to remove anxieties if they are present.

Saturnine sicknesses can be healed by the Sun.

The Sun will give tremendous will power if it is posited in the First House.

The Sun can never be in honour in a female sign.

When the Sun is in fall, it does not show too much of an ego.

The Sun can bring vanity.

The Sun can increase one's physical strength. With the sun rising (on the ascendant or in the First House), the native will have a good constitution, unless there are indications to the contrary.

A transit of the Sun has an influence for three days.

The Sun in Aries favours leadership.

The Sun in Cancer brings luck, since Cancer is a beneficial sign and Jupiter is its ruler by exaltation.

The Sun in trine with Jupiter is a beneficial combination and will bring greatness. If the Sun and Jupiter are each in a good zodiacal state, such a trine will bring good luck.

For a spiritual approach, the Sun is twice as important as the Moon, since it is the ruler of the cardinal sign through exaltation (Aries), while the Moon is the ruler of a fixed sign through exaltation (Taurus).

Light is the natural remedy for afflictions caused by the Sun.

☽ THE MOON

The Moon is the satellite of the Earth. It is the strongest of the lights during the night.

The Moon is between the Earth (the receiver) and Heaven. It is closest to the Earth.

The Moon is a receiver; it is cold and humid. Its orb is 17 degrees.

The Moon never appears retrograde.

The general significator of the mother is the Moon. It is very important to have a wise mother.

In the horoscope of a man, the Moon can also represent older women.

The Moon represents emotions and the instincts (unconscious), which come from the cerebellum. The emotions depend on the unconscious. Most problems come from the unconscious.

The goal of life is to satisfy the instincts. An instinct is either a healthy one or an unhealthy one. A person with unhealthy instincts should be prevented from harming others. Most people do not have their instincts developed strongly enough. The instinct of a woman who desires children should be used in the selection of a father.

Survival is an instinct.

When the Moon is in a bad zodiacal state, the instincts will be bad. However, one can train oneself to go against one's bad instincts and to improve them. Whatever is connected with the emotions can be a source of difficulty, because it is not always easy to channel the emotions in a constructive way, i.e., to find the right outlet.

> He who was heedless but who now is restrained and reflective is like the moon freed from a cloud; he brightens the world.
>
> —The Dhammapada: The World 6(172)

Until the age of seven, children are connected with the Moon. The public is connected with the Moon.

The Moon gives compassion.

The position of the Moon in a specific horoscope represents the horizon at the time of conception. There are ten lunar months from conception to birth.

The prenatal horoscope does not necessarily coincide with the biological conception, but with the incarnation of the soul.

Memory is connected with the Moon.

> Memory is the not letting go of an object that one has been aware of.
>
> —Patanjali, Book I:11

For good judgement you need an excellent Moon.

Intuition is usually connected with the Moon. You can improve your intuition by learning and practicing telepathy, clairvoyance, and precognition.

Dreams indicate an active unconscious. In a general way, dreams are connected with the Moon and Neptune. The Moon and Neptune are planets that bring imagination.

> By dwelling on knowledge that presents itself in a dream, steadiness of mind may be procured.
>
> —Patanjali, Book I:38

In terms of everyday life, the Moon is twice as important as the Sun, since it is the ruler of a cardinal sign (Cancer), while the Sun is the ruler of a fixed sign (Leo).

If, in a horoscope, the Moon is unimportant, e.g., in a cadent house and in a mutable sign, and if the majority of the planets are in male signs, there will be no instincts.

The Moon in an airy sign shows intelligence and communication, and can prove very beneficial. One's degree of intelligence is connected with the rising sign and with the Moon. The Moon in Scorpio shows that the unconscious is too strongly connected with the sex drive.

The Moon can never be in honour in a male sign, since no male sign can understand the Moon.

Water is the natural remedy for afflictions caused by the Moon.

The Sun and the Moon

A distinction must be made between personality and individuality. Each human being is a person. If a person evolves, he becomes an individual. Personality is connected with the Moon and does not have a great value. A person with a prominent Moon in his horoscope relies heavily on other people. Individuality is connected with the Sun. The Sun gives high values. The more we use the conscious, the more we confront consciousness and higher values. The true individual has an inner drive and relies on his higher self, towards which he learns to attune himself. However, to achieve this without losing one's ethics is very difficult, since, in order to survive, a person might be tempted to lower his values at given times. Every planet helps the realization of the Sun (the spirit) and the Moon (the soul). You can change your personality by increasing the influence of a particular planet. You can also change your personality through diet, a lowering of tensions through autogenic training, sound sleep, and by changing your breathing habits.

The Sun should be connected with the Moon by an aspect. The aspect may be either harmonious or disharmonious, but the important thing is that they be connected to enable the realization of the instincts. The forces of the soul must cooperate with those of the spirit. An incarnation should aim at the evolution of the soul, otherwise there is no true evolution. The Sun must be inspired by the Moon.

If the Sun and the Moon are in male signs, there will be a difficulty in bringing out the unconscious. If both are in female signs, it will be easy.

When both lights are in the same sign, we call it a new moon, and there will be a psychological problem, due to one of the lights overpowering the other. If the Sun and the Moon are in male signs, the Sun will overpower the Moon, since the Sun is masculine and is therefore the stronger of the two in the male sign. The reverse would be true if both of the lights were in the same female sign.

When both lights and the ruler of the ascendant are below the horizon, the native is said to have been born during a "dark night," and the horoscope should be considered weak. Weakness means having no goal or ability to realize one's desires, and/or no strength to fight the environment, since, as it has been stated previously, astrology is connected with the time of birth and with the environment. It is better to have one of the lights above the horizon.

An opposition between the Sun and the Moon is called a full Moon and may be considered dangerous. It brings a struggle between the conscious and the unconscious, but it is better to struggle and to fail than not to struggle at all. An opposition can prove to be very constructive, however, if there is an interfering planet, i.e., a planet that sends a beneficial aspect to one or both of the planets involved in the opposition.

> For everyone who has, more will be given, and he will have abundance;
> but from him who has not, even what he has will be taken away.
>
> —Matthew 25:29

A conjunction between the Sun and the Moon can be difficult. It is not favorable psychologically.

A square aspect between the Sun and the Moon can be very dangerous, since insoluble problems can be created between the conscious and the unconscious. Square aspects reflect dissatisfaction. In this case, one should look at the influence of Saturn (the guardian of the threshold). The interference of Saturn would weaken the acceleration (disharmony) caused by the square. A square between the Sun and the Moon is not bad if you have the courage to fight and the will to fulfil the drive of the Moon in a civilized way. What each person needs is a good Moon, giving a good instinctive drive. For spiritual evolution, the Sun is more important than the Moon, because the Sun is in exaltation in an angular house of the zodiac (Aries), and the Moon is in exaltation in a succedent house (Taurus). Thus, the Sun, by position, is stronger. The realization of the instincts has to do with the Sun. When the instincts cannot be directed through the Sun, there will be involution. In the context of time, the day serves to realize the night. The astrological day should start in the evening and go until the next evening. There are four possibilities:

1. The Sun and Moon are both strong.

2. The Sun is strong and the Moon is weak.

3. The Sun is weak and the Moon is strong.

4. The Sun and the Moon are both weak.

There are three possible aspects between the Sun and the Moon:

1. The Sun and the Moon are in a good aspect (trine or sextile). These harmonious aspects, however, may not produce enough drive.

2. The Sun and the Moon are in a disharmonious aspect, a square indicating acceleration, or an opposition indicating retardation.

3. There is no aspect between the Sun and the Moon. In this case, there is no desire or drive to solve a problem or to realize the unconscious. The exception to this would be if both lights are in honour. In that case, no aspect is needed. When the two lights are in exaltation, it can cause one to go to the extremes; there can be too much of a desire to be perfect.

On the physical plane you need a good father and a happy mother.

To have a mother in the world is happiness, to have a father in the world is happiness.

—The Dhammapada: The Elephant 13(332)

Do we choose our parents? The answer to this should be that our knowledge at this stage of evolution is insufficient.

In the zodiac, Saturn (ruler of Capricorn and co-ruler of Aquarius) is the planet that opposes both the Moon (Cancer) and the Sun (Leo), the symbols of life. The Sun and the Moon give life, but Saturn suppresses it. The Sun and the Moon can be free from Saturn's influence, if Saturn's influence is used for a profession, since in the archetype, Saturn is the ruler of the house of destiny, career, profession, etc. Choose your profession carefully. A way for some people to escape the melancholia caused by Saturn's influence is to get married.

The Planets

Every planet helps the realization of the two lights, the Sun and the Moon.

A planet radiates, or sends, influences. A planet is in eight places simultaneously: bodily by its position and by aspect in seven other places (two sextiles, two squares, two trines, and one opposition). A planet transits either over a place occupied by another planet or over an unoccupied place.

A planet may or may not accentuate harmony.

Each planet is good and bad at the same time, good for something and bad for something else. Planets influence us according to the way in which we receive their influences. A planet behaves according to its own nature and according to its zodiacal state. In general, planets in male signs tend to show strength. Planets in female signs tend to show weakness.

Each planet must cooperate with the ruler (called the dispositor) of the sign in which it is posited.

Every sign is the domicile of a particular planet.

A planet may or may not help to realize that which a house signifies.

A planet posited 5 degrees or less before the cusp of a house works for that house.

A planet should have an average speed: not too fast and not too slow. If a planet is retrograde, it is too slow, and it may cause a person to change his mind, his direction, and to give up his goals. A retrograde planet is weak and is less practical than one that is direct in motion.

The planet that is the ruler of your ascendant should be studied first.

With each planet, you must see where it is (in which house and sign), from where it comes (which house it rules), where it goes (to the house in which its ruler, called the dispositor, is found), and where the ruler of the dispositor (called the final dispositor) is posited and where it rules. The ruler of a house is the ruler of the sign on the cusp of the house you are examining.

A planet starts an action, its dispositor takes it over, and the final dispositor finishes it. This means that a planet is influential for approximately the first third of life before its dispositor takes over in influence. However, this is not a hard and fast rule. It is only a generalization. For example, if the first planet is in a fixed sign, its influence will be maintained for a very long time.

In a birth chart, the planet closest by aspect to either the ascendant or the mid-heaven is the planet of greatest importance (influence).

Planets in male signs are active.

Planets in female signs are reactive.

A planet is stronger in conjunction with another than in opposition to another.

The conjunction is Mercurial in nature. It is a retarding or an accelerating force, depending upon the promissor and the significator. In the case of a conjunction between Saturn and Mercury, one should determine if either is the ruler of the ascendant. For instance, if Mercury is the significator (i.e., the ruler of the ascendant) and Saturn is the promissor, Saturn will dull the intelligence of Mercury.

An opposition is Saturnine in nature, and represents retardation and/or isolation. In the zodiac, Saturn, the ruler of the tenth sign, representing one's career and destiny, is in opposition to the Moon, the ruler of the fourth sign, representing one's home. Saturn, the ruler by exaltation of the seventh sign, representing one's partners, is also in opposition to Mars, the ruler of the first sign, representing one's physical and mental constitution.

The trine is of the nature of Jupiter, and is two-thirds as strong in influence as the opposition.

The square is of the nature of Mars and is half as strong in influence as the opposition. The square causes acceleration and produces tension. One should fight to build a profession and a home. This fight can be seen in the square aspect, which occurs between each of these two houses (the Tenth and Fourth Houses) and the ascendant in the archetype.

The sextile is one-third as strong as the opposition and is of the nature of Venus. Venus loves and does not fight like Mars.

A planet has an influence of 100 percent when posited in an angular house, 50 percent in a succedent house, and 25 percent in a cadent house.

If the ruler of the ascendant is in an angular house, it is very powerful.

Fixed stars correspond to planets in their nature. To assess the influence of fixed stars, one must consider:

a) the planets that are connected with them; if they are of the same nature, the power drive of the planet involved will be enhanced.
b) the orb of the conjunction between the fixed star and the planet.

c) the magnitude of the fixed star, i.e., a fixed star of first magnitude will eventually exert its influence in a wider orb, but not exceeding 3-4 degrees.

When all of the planets in a horoscope are in honour and are connected, the native will be evolved, with values of a higher nature, either for daily life or for spiritual life. A planet in honour causes things to be achieved in a constructive way. Planets in dishonour produce inferior values.

If a planet is in an intercepted sign, which indicates that there is a distortion in the horoscope, its influence will not be as strong. A distorted horoscope can produce a disharmonious approach to life.

When more than one planet is in a sign, the one nearest the cusp of a house will be strongest in influence, unless one of the planets is in honour, in which case that planet becomes strongest.

The planets receive influences from the zodiac, and, in this regard, are feminine in nature.

The planets send influences to the Earth, and, in this regard, are masculine in nature.

Each planet is connected with one of the five senses. Uranus, Neptune, and Pluto (the "modern" planets) should be connected with higher forces i.e., those senses beyond the five. Uranus represents the sixth sense, Neptune the seventh sense (the third eye), and Pluto the eighth.

The "modern" planets are called the higher octaves of the planets underlying them. Only if the underlying planets are in a good zodiacal state, will the quality of the modern planet be good. Uranus is the higher octave of Mercury. Neptune is the higher octave of Venus. Pluto is the higher octave of Mars.

Strong modern planets in the horoscopes of people born in the twentieth century are in conformity with modern times. The modern planets (Uranus, Neptune, and Pluto) were discovered relatively recently. Astrology is a science based on observation. We still know too little about the modern planets in order to be able to extend the meaning and the implications (repercussions) of zodiacal state (such as exaltation) to them.

Uranus can give tremendous intelligence.

Neptune is believed to work with the unconscious and to give imagination.

Pluto can give clear vision.

As of this writing, scientists are still searching for a transplutonian planet.

Modern planets are especially influential in the horoscopes of innovative persons. They open the way to higher perceptions.

The part of fortune that is associated with one's finances, material fortunes, possessions, and health is not a sender. The nodes of the Moon are not senders but receivers. However, the primary receivers are the ascendant, the mid-heaven, and the cusps of the other houses.

In order for the Moon's nodes to have an influence, they must be connected with a planet through a conjunction. The orb should not be wider than one degree.

The strong significance of the nodes in Indian astrology can be taken either seriously or as superstition.

The north node of the Moon is connected with Jupiter and Venus, and the south node is connected with Saturn and Mars.

When the majority of the planets are in the eastern half of the chart, it signifies a tremendous need for the native to bring out something in himself. (A good example of this can be seen in the birth chart of Morin de Villefranche, the French astrologer of the sixteenth century.) It signifies a concern with oneself and, thus, self-centeredness.

When the majority of the planets are in the western half of the horoscope, it signifies a concern for others.

Four planets or more in a sign (a stellium) have more influence than the Fourth House (the parents). In a stellium, the planet in domicile is the most important. Generally, a stellium is not desirable because it is disharmonious (too much), but for evolution, disharmony functions as a drive and may prove very beneficial (as in the birth chart of Louis Pasteur). A stellium in a mutable sign shows lack of will.

Too many planets in the same sign can bring confusion, especially when in the sign of Sagittarius.

In the case where all planets are below the horizon, the native will be introverted and not very active.

Zodiacal State of Planets

The first thing to look at is a planet's zodiacal state. The advantageous zodiacal states are exaltation, domicile, and honour of triplicity. The disadvantageous zodiacal states are detriment and fall. When a planet is in a good zodiacal state it is said to be in honour. When a planet is in a bad zodiacal state, it is said to be in dishonour. A planet in dishonour is not advantageous. If, in a horoscope, all planets are in honour and no planets are in dishonour, generally speaking whatever the native does will bring success.

If a planet, by nature a helper (i.e., a benefic—Venus or Jupiter), is in a good zodiacal state, it will bring good fortune.

Good means beneficial for your future, and bad means destructive for your future. A planet may be bad by its nature (a malefic—Mars or Saturn), through its zodiacal state, or through its disharmonious aspects to other planets. Bad means also too much or too little. Thus, it is possible for a good planet to harm by overdoing. "Nothing in excess" was engraved at the entrance to the Temple of Apollo at Delphi in Ancient Greece.

Masculine planets give extroversion, while feminine ones give introversion.

The influence of a planet results from both its quality and its quantity.

The quality of a planet is determined by its nature. The nature of the Sun and Mars is warm and dry. Jupiter and Venus are warm and humid. The Moon is cold and humid, and Saturn and Mercury are cold and dry.

The zodiacal state is more important than the nature of a planet. Planets in a bad zodiacal state can cause a person to become pushy and inclined to have materialistic values. Planets in a good zodiacal state incline a person to have ethical values. The zodiacal state of planets is affected by the aspects that the planets receive. Lack of harmony, even with planets in a good zodiacal state, is not good, and detracts from the quality of the zodiacal state. Being too nice may be considered an example of a lack of harmony. If you are too nice, you may become a victim.

> "Hard is the life for one who is modest,
> who always seeks for what is pure,
> who is disinterested, unassuming, chaste
> and has insight."
>
> —The Dhammapada: Impurity 7(245)

The quantity of a planet is also important. If, for instance, Mars is connected with other malefic planets through bad aspects, the quantity of Mars may increase to the point of being dangerous. If you don't have the right quantity, you will choose people without quality.

He who consorts with fools, experiences great grief.

—The Dhammapada: Happiness 11(207)

The company of fools is like the company of enemies—productive of pain.

—The Dhammapada: Happiness 11(207)

Retrograde planets are 10 percent less powerful in quantity than planets that are direct in motion, and they are less practical. The Sun and the Moon (the lights) are never retrograde.

A planet in an angular house can cause overcompensation. Each house cusp has a 5 degree orb on either side of it. A planet in one house, 5 degrees near the cusp of the next house, will influence that next house, but only on the psychological level, not on the physical level.

One's power drive will be greater when there are planets connected with the ascendant (the personality) or with the mid-heaven (the realization of the personality and of the profession), either bodily or by aspect. If by aspect, the more exact it is, the greater the drive will be.

A planet in honour achieves things in a constructive way. The values of a planet in a good zodiacal state are on a more spiritual level than those of a planet in a bad zodiacal state. If a planet is in a good zodiacal state, what is obtained or achieved will bring happiness.

When the planets are in a bad zodiacal state, the values will be more materialistic. A planet in dishonour can produce a very negative attitude. One may achieve things but, unless by overcompensating one exercises the right judgement, one will achieve things in the wrong way, and what is achieved will be the source of unhappiness. Freedom is taken away by planets in a bad zodiacal state.

Evil tendencies of the unrestrained and careless go on increasing if they neglect doing what ought to be done and do that which ought not to be done.

—The Dhammapada: Miscellaneous 3(292)

A planet in domicile is excellent for earthly affairs, where it gives ethical values. Even when a planet that is malefic by nature (i.e., Saturn or Mars) is in domicile, it cannot harm too much.

A planet in exaltation reflects very high spiritual values, but the exaltation gives no advantages on the human level. For example, the Sun in Aries may even give arrogance.

An exalted planet can be dangerous in that it functions well only on

46

a spiritual level. Exaltation is appreciated in the Orient, but, in the West exaltation is considered to cause neurosis. Exaltation goes for purity, and a person with planets in exaltation may have difficulty in adjusting to daily life.

> Like a thoroughbred horse touched by a whip, let a man be ardent and active; By faith and virtue, energy and mind, by discernment of the law, endowed with knowledge, good behaviour, concentrated, he will strike off the great sorrow of earthly existence.

> —The Dhammapada: The Rod of Punishment: 10(144)

Exaltation is connected with evolution because it increases the values of the conscious. A bad Moon (for example, a full Moon in Capricorn or in Scorpio) destroys the values of the conscious.

When planets are in exaltation, money can mean very little, particularly when the native's country is strongly connected with religious ideas.

A planet in exaltation, or even in its domicile, might signify too much of a task to fulfil. It will mean evolvement from the physical world to the spiritual world.

In India, a horoscope with three planets in exaltation is considered to be a very evolved horoscope. In the West a person with an evolved horoscope will have the urge to go beyond the limits of his environment, by contributing to its welfare.

> To do good work is noble. To urge others to do good work is even more noble . . . and it isn't very hard.

> —Mark Twain

The most desirable zodiacal state for planets for the average person is "honour of triplicity," because it represents neither too much nor too little of the qualities involved. If the ruler of the ascendant is not in honour of triplicity, other signs might become more important than the sign on the ascendant.

The zodiacal state of peregrine creates an attitude of indifference and shows retardation. Peregrinity is not constructive. The word peregrine means to wander. Peregrine planets do not stick to one thing.

The most important house in a horoscope is the First House, but the most influential house is the Tenth (the ruler of destiny).

As a rule, people use the Moon, Mercury, Venus, and Mars in their daily lives. The Sun (the will) is not always used.

If the majority of the planets, including the Moon, are under the horizon there will be introversion. There will also be magnetism, but magnetism brings suffering.

Planetary Influences

A person receives the influences of planets in a good or in a bad way, but good and bad must be qualified, since what is good for something may be bad for something else and vice versa. An intelligent human being knows how to decrease the effects of bad planetary influences. As it has been said previously, the more you evolve, the more you become responsible.

The rising sign, or ascendant, cannot be changed during life. You have to see what planetary influences (aspects) your ascendant is receiving, and what influences (aspects) the ruler of your ascendant is receiving, in order to assess the native's physical and mental constitution.

The quality of a planetary influence is very important, but more important is the quantity of the planetary influence, because the real power of a planet is connected with its quantity.

Planetary influences can be changed, but we must accept limitations. The wise man will accept limitations as a blessing. "In limitation we find the Master." The birth chart shows the behaviour pattern of a person.

Limitation is wisdom. To ask for too much means dissatisfaction, and that is the end of wisdom. Saturn seeks limitations whereas Mars and Pluto do not.

Quantity and quality are disregarded if a planet is not connected either with the ascendant or the midheaven. One's power drive will be greater when planets are connected with the ascendant and/or with the mid-heaven. Planetary influences are increased through transits.

Planetary Influences are determined by:

1. *Position:* in what house and in what sign. (The nature of a planet and its zodiacal state cannot be changed.) A planet is of maximum importance when close either to the ascendant or to the mid-heaven. As a rule, a planet in an angular house is very powerful, more powerful than in a succedent or cadent house.

2. *Disposition:* the ruler of the sign in which a planet is posited is called its dispositor. The final dispositor is the dispositor of the dis-

positor. Each planet must cooperate with its dispositor and also with the ruler of the dispositor. The position of the ruler of the dispositor must be taken into account.

3. **Aspects:** The word aspect comes from the Latin *'aspecto,'* which means 'to look at.' Aspects between the signs show quality, while aspects between the planets show quantity. Within one sign, there is the aspect called a conjunction. (For a true conjunction, the planets must be in the same sign.) Aspects involving two signs include the Venusian sextile, the Martian square, the Jupiterian trine, the Saturnine opposition, and the Neptunian quincunx. The good (harmonious) aspects are the trine and the sextile. With a trine, for example, you are lucky, but only if there is a drive. The bad (disharmonious) aspects are the square and the opposition. A bad aspect brings a person down to the earthly world. The exactness of the aspect in terms of degrees between planets gives the quantity. Quantity is also shown by the house position. Quality is shown by the zodiacal state. In order to determine accurately the influence of the aspects in a horoscope, one must consider the age of the native, because it determines the way the native will receive the planetary influences, hence their aspects.

The influence of a planet is strongest in the aspects of conjunction and opposition, two-thirds as strong in a trine, half as strong in a square, and one-third as strong in a sextile.

Aspects can help or destroy, depending upon the planets involved and their zodiacal states. In an aspect, the influence of the receiving planet is more important than that of the sending one. To determine which is the receiving planet and which is the sending one will depend upon the house you are examining. The planets of the house under study are the receiving ones. Aspects should be judged by the planets that form them, and in relation to their dispositors. Aspects are either dexter (running from right to left, against the order of the signs of the zodiac—clockwise) or sinister (running from left to right in the order of the zodiac—counterclockwise); e.g., Pluto in Cancer receives a dexter square from Venus in Libra and a sinister square from Mars in Aries.

An aspect is said to be too harmonious if there is not enough drive. Thus, an aspect between two planets is harmonious only if there is not too much or too little.

There are four possibilities with aspects between planets:

A. between two beneficial planets in a good zodiacal state;

B. between two beneficial planets in bad zodiacal state (in this case, the aspect might prove to be a small destroyer);

C. between two malefic planets in good zodiacal state (in this case, the aspect might prove to be a small helper);

D. between two malefic planets in bad zodiacal state.

In general, an aspect between two planets in dishonour will cause misfortune.

If, in a horoscope, there is no opposition between any two planets, there could be too much activity (uncontrolled activity).

If all planets are above the horizon, there will be no oppositions, and the native will be extroverted and overactive.

If all planets are below the horizon, there will be no oppositions, and the native will be introverted and not sufficiently active.

An opposition is excellent if there is an interfering planet and if one of the two lights is below the horizon. An interfering planet is a third planet that sends either a sextile or a trine to one of the planets in the opposition. This planet, in effect, "solves" the opposition. Since the ascendant and the mid-heaven are not senders but only receivers, the ascendant and the mid-heaven cannot solve an opposition.

A horoscope without oppositions shows no struggle.

If, in the natal horoscope, there is a sextile between two planets, and in a lunar revolution there is a square between the same planets there will be an acceleration because the nature of the square is to accelerate. The reverse will occur if there is an opposition in a lunar revolution with the same planets; in such a case, there will be a retardation, because the nature of the opposition is to delay.

Planets in a mutual reception can be advantageous in a square or an opposition, e.g., Venus in a Martian sign opposed or squared by Mars in a Venusian sign.

A square aspect shows dissatisfaction. Too much is desired in too little time. The square indicates building up, fighting, and impatience. Impatience is resistance to knowledge.

A T-square (two planets in opposition forming squares with a third one) is not a favourable aspect.

A quincunx (150 degrees) is not considered one of the major aspects. It is Neptunian in nature, bringing indifference and lack of clarity. It causes a retardation, resulting from a karmic situation. A quincunx aspect between the cusp of the Fifth House and the ascendant indicates that Fifth House affairs will be neglected.

Half-sextile aspects are considered minor aspects and are good for half a year (PISTIS SOPHIAS).

4. ***Ricochet:*** is the term used to describe the action of a planet in one house influencing the opposite house.

Problems

Problems are caused by the malefics (Saturn and Mars), most notably through the quantity of their influence as rulers of angular houses in the archetype, but also from squares and oppositions involving these planets.

When you have a problem, you should try to solve it (not trying would reflect a fatalistic attitude), but you have to know what method to use that will not have a negative repercussion.

Deadly Sins

The "Seven Deadly Sins" are connected with bad aspects between different houses and the planets therein. (As stated previously, bad stands for too much or too little.) These sins (pride, envy, sloth, intemperance, avarice, ire, and lust) involve action or conduct characterized by a violation of divine law, entailing spiritual death.

Pride: is connected with a bad aspect between the Sun and Jupiter. Conversely, a good aspect between the Sun and Jupiter will show greatness.

A man's pride brings him low, but a man of a lowly spirit gains honour.

—Proverbs 29:23

Love one another with brotherly affection, outdo one another in showing honour.

—Romans 12:10

Envy: is always connected with malefics. Saturn will cause envy on the material plane, e.g., exaggerated desire for money, and Mars will cause envy on the emotional plane, e.g., exaggerated emotions and/or sex drive.

Craving grows in a disturbed mind, also when passions flourish, and when
yearnings for the pleasant arise. Thus fetters grow strong.

—The Dhammapada: Craving 16(399)

Jealousy: is a form of anxiety and is often connected with Saturn.
It is not always connected with love. To stop loving is not possible. Loving
means giving. The pathway to love is through forgiveness. Seldom does
one understand love. Research of various civilizations has proved that
the relationship between male and female cannot be solved.

You shall not covet your neighbour's house . . . or anything that belongs to
your neighbour.

—Exodus 20:17

Greed: results from anxiety and reflects a combination of Mars and
Saturn (square or opposition).

He who is greedy for unjust gains makes trouble, but he who hates bribes
will live.

—Proverbs 15:27

A rich man is inclined to become greedy and should give a part of
his fortune away.

> Blessed is he who considers the poor!
> The Lord delivers him in the day of trouble.

—Psalm 41:1

For anyone who eats and drinks without discerning the body, eats and
drinks judgment upon himself. That is why many of you are weak and ill,
and some have died.

—1 Corinthians 11:29,30

Violence: is caused by an excess quantity of Mars, resulting in
anger and passion. Anger is a projection of one's guilty fears. One has
to learn to dissolve resentment and to choose only happy thoughts.

Fury's sounds mean nothing.

—Shakespeare

He who is slow to anger has great understanding, but he who has a hasty temper exalts fully.

—Proverbs 14:29

Lying: is connected with a bad Jupiter, but if you lie in the interest of another person it should not be considered lying.

Lying lips are an abomination to the Lord but those who act faithfully are his delight.

—Proverbs 12:22

The Lord detests lying lips, but He delights in men who are truthful.

—Proverbs 12:22

Self-Control

In order to determine how much self-control a person has, you must study in particular the ascendant, the Sun, the signs that are above the horizon, and the aspects. Self-control is indicated when the ascendant (physical and mental constitution) and the Sun (the will) and their rulers are in a good zodiacal state and well aspected. It also depends upon the number of male signs that are above the horizon and upon aspects between planets, i.e., Saturn in trine with the Moon. Self-control does not necessarily require self-criticism, which should be avoided as an extreme. Self-criticism intensifies problems. Be kind and gentle to yourself. The other extreme would be unscrutinized self-acceptance and self-approval.

A man without self-control is like a city broken into and left without walls.

—Proverbs 25:28

Significators and Promissors

The zodiac reflects the general, and a natal or birth horoscope the particular. Each planet may be a significator or a promissor. The native is signified in his horoscope by a planet (known as the significator), and events are promised by another planet (known as the promissor). The promissor conforms its nature to the age and the sex of the native. It "promises," by aspect, something to the significator. A promissor is connected with a house and the planets in it. If the promissor is in a good zodiacal state, the values will be high.

A significator is either general (as when in the Zodiac) or particular (as when in a birth horoscope).

Mercury is the general significator of intelligence, study, writing, correspondence, and travel. It rules the arms, legs, hands, feet, tongue, and the thyroid gland.

Venus is the general significator of love, art, music, and drama, as well as of social functions. Venus, a benefic, is also the promissor of these things. It rules the kidneys.

Mars is the general significator of passion, war, violence, accident, and of sudden destruction. It rules the male sex organs.

Jupiter is the general significator of good fortune. It is also the general promissor of wisdom, and it rules the liver.

Saturn is the general significator of foresight, limitation, negation, and isolation. It rules the bones and the skin.

Planetary Interferences

In order to interpret a horoscope, everything has to be taken into consideration. An astrologer must always study the archetype, namely, the zodiac, and must compare the birth horoscope with the archetype. Whatever in a birth chart is a duplication of the zodiac is good.

An astrologer must look for what are known as "interferences" in a horoscope; these must be studied carefully, since they greatly affect the interpretation of a horoscope. Science, specifically medicine, may be considered an interference, even though it is not within the birth chart, because it can interfere with sicknesses. Education or the lack thereof is yet another example of an interference.

The most important interference is seen in aspects to the horizon. If, for instance, a person is born with Leo rising, but shows himself to lack will power, we must look for an interference. Too many interferences cause difficulties. All interferences retard evolution. (However, evolution should not necessarily be accelerated.)

"Don't push too hard at the beginning."

One must see if there are influences that compete with the ascendant and/or mid-heaven, or influences that cooperate with and are enhancing either of these or both.

☿ MERCURY

Mercury, a planet of the mutable (common) cross, is of the nature of Saturn; it is cold and dry.

Because of its proximity to the Sun, Mercury is superficial; it cannot go into depth and is always lost in details. It is very versatile and practical and likes to serve.

Mercury is the planet of intelligence (the mind), analysis, flexibility, communication, technology, and the nervous system. It rules the lungs, the thyroid gland, and the eyes, and is closely allied with external vision. When there is a legal battle, you must study Mercury.

Mercury is in domicile by day in Gemini and by night in Virgo. It is in detriment in Sagittarius and in Pisces. In Pisces it is also in fall. It is in honour of triplicity in Taurus, Libra, Aquarius, and Capricorn, and peregrine in Aries, Cancer, Leo, and Scorpio. Mercury is in exaltation, as well as in domicile, in the sign of Virgo. If Mercury, as ruler of the ascendant, is in Virgo, it may be a disadvantage for the native, because Mercury is restless in Virgo.

A person is under the influence of Mercury from the age of seven to fourteen. In astrology, Mercury represents the tree of knowledge. Sheer knowledge (intelligence) is the enemy of wisdom (Jupiter). Mercury, lower in its position in the Zodiac than Jupiter, cannot see the higher (Jupiter). The word intelligence means literally, "I understand." Wisdom means belief in God (Ninth House), in one's Karma (Twelfth House), and the acceptance of suffering. Mercury always wants to outsmart Jupiter; thus, a good aspect between these two planets will hardly bring the usual practical benefits of good aspects.

The lips of the righteous know what is acceptable but the mouth of the wicked, what is perverse.

—Proverbs 10:32

Mercury in the Ninth House in detriment is unfavourable for metaphysics.

A good Mercury has the right amount of speed. In order to determine a planet's speed, you should look at the daily motion of the planet, the sign it is in, and whether or not it is retrograde. Mercury in Gemini is fast. Mercury in an earthy sign is slow. If Mercury is retrograde, the mind will not be quick and will be less practical.

The zodiacal state of Mercury in a birth chart indicates how well organized the native is. In a good zodiacal state, Mercury functions as an advantageous planetary influence. Mercury is especially good when it is connected with many planets and with the lights.

Intelligence has a secret enemy: money (as represented by the Second House in the archetype). However, you need money in order to have friends.

In Greek mythology, Mercury (Hermes) was the messenger of the Gods. He came down to the earth in order to teach writing, music, and science. In Egyptian mythology, Mercury was called TOTH. Mercury is not a strong planet in comparison to the other planets. The true nature of Mercury is mischievous, restless, and malevolent. It is a planet of perversion. The more Mercurial you become, the more unhappy you are apt to become, because the will and the soul become servants of the mind.

The soul is conjoined in the body with the organ of thought.

—Patanjali, Book II:17

In him who knows the difference between the nature of the soul and mind, the false notion regarding the soul comes to an end.

—Patanjali, Book IV:24

To watch the mind is conducive to happiness.

—The Dhammapada: The Mind 4:36

One's practical intelligence does not work when Mercury is in detriment or in fall. That is why Mercury is not good in Pisces (the sign of compassion), where it is both in detriment and in fall. With Mercury in Pisces, reality becomes distorted. Mercury is in detriment also in Sagittarius, the sign of wisdom. The following story is an example of a cunning mercurial mind:

A man who had committed a murder stood before a judge along with two witnesses who had seen the murder. The murderer pleaded with the judge to pardon him, saying that he could bring a thousand witnesses who had not seen him commit the crime, each of whom would testify that he did not do it.

Mercurial people calculate. Agents of all kinds are mercurial. A prostitute often has a bad Mercury. A prostitute can put aside all of her emotions and function only on the physical level.

> For the lips of a loose woman drip honey, and her speech is smoother than oil; but in the end she is bitter as wormwood, sharp as a two-edged sword.
>
> —Proverbs 5:3,4

A truly Mercurial attitude will be amoral. If somebody says, "Let me tell you the truth," the Mercurial answer might be, "Who needs it?"

Mercury in the Seventh House indicates that the native will be connected with the public.

A Mercurial affliction can be alleviated by healing the mind.

In order to be a scientist, one should have a good Mercury, well connected with Saturn. Philosophers should have a good Mercury, well connected with Jupiter.

Good Communication

> The wise of heart is called man of discernment and pleasant speech increases persuasiveness.
>
> —Proverbs 16:21

> Pleasant words are like honeycomb, sweetness to the soul and health to the body.
>
> —Proverbs 16:27

Aspects of Mercury

A bad aspect between Mercury and the Moon brings a dangerous conflict between the intelligence and the unconscious. (Bruno Hauptman, the murderer of Charles Lindbergh's son, had an exact square between Mercury and the Moon.) In the case of a square between Mercury and the Moon, the instinctive desires of the Moon cannot be realized; because of Mercury, the instincts break down. However, when Mercury is in a good aspect with the Moon, what you want instinctively is facilitated via Mercury.

A good aspect between Mercury and Uranus (Uranus being the

higher octave of Mercury) will speed up the nervous system. A bad aspect between Mercury and Uranus may produce too much speed, especially if it is a square. An astrologer should have a good connection between Mercury and Uranus, enabling him to break away from old-fashioned thinking. Awareness is the key to change. One must get rid of resistance to change and learn to take life in an easy-going way. The future is shaped on the present.

A person with a conjunction between Mercury and Uranus will think very quickly and will have an unusual mind.

With a trine between Mercury and Jupiter, there may be strong tendencies to reform and educate the masses.

With a conjunction between Mercury and Saturn, one should determine which is the significator and which is the promissor. If Saturn is the significator, ways and means will be found to solve problems, but there will be a tendency to be antisocial because Saturn isolates. Generally, Saturn conjunct Mercury produces heaviness or sluggishness of the mind.

With a conjunction between Mercury and Neptune, fantasy will have no limits. With Mercury in opposition to Neptune, the truth may be skillfully evaded and uncreditable acts may be rationalized.

With a square between Mercury and Pluto, the mind should be kept as flexible as possible, since Pluto represents events that are beyond our control and causes deep-rooted fears of the unconscious. According to the astrologer Charles Vougas, mental flexibility demands avoidance in the process of thinking of any dryness, overcondensation and all subtle forms of stubbornness.

♀ VENUS

Venus is the planet of love and beauty. Venus gives not only physical beauty, but also the beauty of the soul. It is a beneficial promissor and can bring happiness. Venus wants to serve through love and likes to help; it does not fight. Love lieth at the foundation. The nature of Venus is warm and humid.

Venus is in:

Day domicile in:	Libra
Night domicile in:	Taurus
Exaltation in:	Pisces

Detriment in:	Aries and Scorpio
Fall in:	Virgo
Honour of triplicity in:	Gemini, Capricorn, Aquarius
Peregrine in:	Cancer, Leo, Sagittarius

Venus governs the affections and social relations. It rules the kidneys.

In a man's horoscope, it represents a younger woman.

A person is under the influence of Venus from the age of fourteen to twenty-one.

What Mars destroys, Venus rebuilds. Venus and Mars each rule masculine, cardinal signs (Libra and Aries).

Venus can signify money, but, in order to have money, one has to overcome one's personality or ego (represented by the First House), which is the hidden enemy of money (represented by the Second House).

If Venus causes affliction to one's health, it will generally be a depletion that may be treated with rest and recreation, but Venus may cause venereal diseases also.

Venus is not connected with the sharpening of the mind.

♂ MARS

Mars is the planet of passion, violence, war, accidents, and sudden destruction. Mars is also the planet of courage, impetuosity, impatience, and rudeness. It is warm and dry. The square aspect is Martian in nature and causes acceleration.

Mars is in:

Day domicile in:	Aries
Night domicile in:	Scorpio
Exaltation in:	Capricorn
Detriment in:	Taurus and Libra. (Mars in Libra is less dangerous than in Taurus.)
Fall in:	Cancer
Honour of triplicity in:	Leo, Sagittarius and Pisces
Peregrine in:	Gemini, Virgo and Aquarius

A person is under the influence of Mars from the age of forty-two to fifty-six.

Nowadays, we need courage (Mars). Mars warms up.

Mars produces the sex drive, thereby helping the preservation of the race.

It stirs the emotions and may provoke them to the point of exaggeration.

Mars can provoke complete lack of foresight. Mars wants to realize its goals without wasting time.

The true Martian acts on first impulse and is never afraid.

An excess of Martian activity will lead to restlessness and lack of tranquility.

An afflicted Mars brings quarrelsomeness or even brutality.

Mars ill-aspected can indicate impetuosity and impatience.

A bad Mars on the ascendant (either in a bad zodiacal state or ill-aspected) may give the tendency for violence. This tendency can be upgraded if, instead of becoming a killer, the native becomes a soldier, a butcher or a surgeon, for example.

A deficiency of Mars can cause shyness, weakness, and indolence.

Headaches are Martian in nature.

Mars is active, insensitive, and goal-oriented.

A man of quick temper acts foolishly but a man of discretion is patient.

—Proverbs 14:17

He who is slow to anger has great understanding, but he who has a hasty temper exalts fully.

—Proverbs 14:29

Fury's sounds mean nothing.

—Shakespeare

Let every man be quick to hear, slow to speak, slow to anger, for the anger of man does not work the righteousness of God.

—James 1:19,20

Mars, exalted in Capricorn, shows activity combined with wisdom.
What Mars destroys, Venus rebuilds.
The left ear belongs to Mars.

In a square between Mars and Pluto, Pluto will accelerate Mars's impetuosity.

♃ JUPITER

Jupiter is a planet of the mutable (common) cross. It is warm and humid.

It is in:

Day domicile in:	Sagittarius
Night domicile in:	Pisces (with Neptune as co-ruler.)
Exaltation in:	Cancer
Detriment in:	Gemini, Virgo
Fall in:	Capricorn
Honour of triplicity in:	Aries, Leo, Scorpio
Peregrine in:	Taurus, Libra, Aquarius

Jupiter is the planet of goodness, of ethics and of wisdom. It is connected with gains, service, and help. It provides enjoyment in life. Jupiter does not give a detail-oriented approach. Rather, it synthesizes.

What Saturn destroys, Jupiter rebuilds. Jupiter protects.

The wisdom of Jupiter dictates the enjoyment of life and a peaceful preparation for death. Jupiter represents optimism and cheerfulness, in contrast to the wisdom of Saturn, which can be summarized: Expect nothing and you will get everything.

One's evolution depends on how he receives his destiny. In the path of destiny, patience has to be cultivated. Is suffering necessary for evolution? The answer is probably "yes," but Jupiter teaches us how to overcome suffering. Jupiter causes one to suffer with dignity.

In the archetype, Jupiter, co-ruler of the Twelfth House (misfortune), is also the ruler of the Ninth House (wisdom). Through derivation, the Ninth House is the Tenth House (the realization) of the Twelfth. By this relationship of cause and effect, we can see that suffering will bring wisdom through Jupiter. That is why it is said that tremendous suffering can give rise to higher evolution.

Jupiter is a giver. In general, wherever you find Jupiter in a horoscope, you find good fortune. In the symbol of Jupiter, the half-moon (the instincts) is above the cross (the materialistic earth). (The symbol of Saturn is the reverse. The cross [the earth] is above the half-moon [the instincts].)

Jupiter rules law and religion.

In order for a person to be truly ethical, his Jupiter must be in a good zodiacal state.

Hence we can confidently say, The Lord is my Helper, I will not be afraid: What can man do to me?

—Hebrews 13: 5,6

Even though I walk through the valley of the shadow of death I fear no evil for thou art with me; thy rod and thy staff, they comfort me.

—Psalm 13:4

Thou dost keep him in perfect peace whose mind is stayed on Thee, because he trusts in Thee.

—Isaiah 16:3

For God did not give us a spirit of timidity but a spirit of power and love and self-control.

—2 Timothy 1:7

You came to the help for those who gladly do right who remember your ways.

—Isaiah 64:5

Jupiter (as well as Venus) is associated with money.

Jupiter rules the liver and, therefore, helps the assimilation of food. A good liver removes toxins. In general, Jupiter can be associated with ailments caused by the wrong diet.

A person is under the influence of Jupiter between the age of fifty-six and sixty-eight.

The planet opposite in nature to Jupiter is Mercury. Accordingly, Jupiter is weak in the Mercurial signs of Gemini and Virgo. Philosophers need a good Jupiter well connected with Mercury.

Jupiter in fall does not reflect the best ethics.

Be not wise in your own eyes: fear the Lord, and turn away from evil. It will be healing to your flesh and refreshment to your bones.

—Proverbs 3:7–8

Jupiter in detriment can indicate immorality.

There are six things which the Lord hates, seven which are an abomination to him; haughty eyes, a lying tongue, and hands that shed innocent blood, a heart that devises wicked plans, feet that make haste to run to evil, a false witness who breathes out lies, and a man who sows discord among brothers.

—Proverbs 6:16–19

Jupiter in the First House increases self-awareness.
Jupiter in Aries gives wisdom.
Jupiter in fall in the Second House may induce one to make money the wrong way (by using unethical means).

He who is greedy for unjust gains makes troubles for his household but he who hates bribes will live.

—Proverbs 15:27

Jupiter in the Seventh House will indicate advantages coming from other people.
Jupiter in the Eighth House can indicate inheritance, money from other people and a peaceful death without suffering. However, in the Middle Ages, Jupiter (which also represents the law) meant death by execution when posited in the Eighth House, as in the horoscope of the son of Cardano, the astrologer of the sixteenth century).
Jupiter in Capricorn in the Ninth House can be indicative of a sophist.

Aspects of Jupiter

The Sun in trine with Jupiter gives greatness. The person who has such a trine will be loved by high-ranking people.

He who is slow to anger is better than the mighty and he who rules his spirit than he who takes a city.

—Proverbs 16:32

63

The best aspect for Jupiter (wisdom) would be a trine to the Moon (the unconscious).

Jupiter (Justice) should be realistic. Therefore, an opposition between Jupiter (law) and Neptune (mercy) is not favourable in that it can create too much leniency.

The only thing necessary for the triumph of evil is for good men to do nothing.

—Edmund Burke

♄ SATURN

According to mythology, Saturn was the father of Jupiter.

An earthy planet, Saturn is cold and dry. It is connected with fate, karma, concentration, and foresight. It can cause nervousness, depression, and anxiety—even an anxiety neurosis. Saturn has been called "The Guardian of the Threshold" (the threshold being between the conscious and the unconscious).

Saturn, the planet of destiny, is associated with a complete lack of free will. It is not a planet of joy and optimism; rather, it is connected with melancholia and pessimism.

The aspect known as the opposition is Saturnine in nature and causes retardation.

Saturn is in:

Day domicile in:	Aquarius
Night domicile in:	Capricorn
Exalted in:	Libra
Detriment in:	Cancer and Leo
Fall in:	Aries
Honour of triplicity in:	Taurus, Gemini, Virgo
Peregrine in:	Scorpio, Sagittarius, Pisces

Saturn is associated with the Tenth House (the house of destiny, profession, and career) because it is the ruler of Capricorn, the sign belonging to this house in the archetype.

Saturn in Capricorn is not good, even though in domicile, because it is too powerful there. Saturn in Capricorn is like a steamroller. The only way to create an outlet for the anxiety that is caused by too strong a Saturn, is to use the anxiety for one's own profit. Saturn in Capricorn is more dangerous than Saturn in Aquarius.

Saturn is the enemy of life; however, without it, there would be overpopulation. It is restrictive by nature and might shorten and suppress life. In the archetype, as ruler of Capricorn and co-ruler of Aquarius, it is opposite to the Moon (ruler of Cancer) and to the Sun (ruler of Leo), the givers of life. It causes decay and degeneration, and can kill by starvation and deterioration.

Saturn often gives psychological loneliness. Loneliness is one of the greatest misfortunes for a person. Jupiter and Mars may help to counteract this.

The true Saturnine approach is one of isolation and pessimism. A hermit is a Saturnine person; he is a man who cannot procreate. A typical Saturnine remark is "I will have to think it over."

One's environment should not be Saturnine. Anxiety and Saturnine sicknesses can be cured by the Sun.

Saturn aims at self-preservation. The urge to stay alive is a healthy instinct. However, self-preservation isolates the individual and too much of a desire for self-preservation is due to anxiety. Saturn can be a helper only through time and patience.

Since Saturn, by nature, stands for limitation, a good Saturn will not allow one to spread out into too many fields of activities at once, so one will not have too many goals at the same time. In limitation we find the Master.

Saturn seeks security, especially material security, i.e., money. It can produce greed.

For the love of money is the root of all evils;

—1 Timothy 6:10

Saturn suppresses the instincts, as does the opposition, an aspect which, as mentioned previously, is of the nature of Saturn.

Saturn can enable a person to have sex without emotion.

Saturn cools down. Wherever you find Saturn in a horoscope, something will be missing. It is the planet of senility. A person is under the influence of Saturn from the age of sixty-eight. The average age of senility is seventy-eight, when the impact of Saturn is tremendous. After the Saturnine period, that is, after the age of seventy-eight, life restarts, in a sense, and we come again under the influence of the Moon, as we were between birth and seven years of age.

The knees, and the bones, in general, are ruled by Saturn.

Saturnine sicknesses include arthritis, cancer, and diseases of the skin and bones. The right ear belongs to Saturn.

Saturn takes away bodily (physical) flexibility. This can be overcome by doing gymnastics, walking outdoors, and taking warm baths. (The Moon gives physical flexibility, and Mercury gives mental flexibility.)

In the chart of an astrologer, Saturn must be strong, because of its role in judgement and foreseeing the future.

A retrograde Saturn is less malefic than a direct Saturn, because it is less strong.

Elements in society that are especially related to Saturn are tradition, conservatism, entrenched authority, and obsolete laws.

Saturn cannot elevate. It limits. In the best case, Saturn gives foresight, such as when there is a trine between the Sun and Saturn. However, foresight can cause anxiety, which can give a fear of time and the feeling that you will not have enough of it in order to achieve your goals. (Buddhists, however, do not worry, because they know they can achieve their goals in future incarnations.) In the worst cases, Saturn produces an inability to work without destruction, such as when there is a square or opposition between Mars and Saturn.

Saturn, by nature, is not generous. It is not a spendthrift, and it is never foolish.

> Therefore do not be anxious about tomorrow for tomorrow will be anxious for itself. Let the day's own trouble be sufficient for the day.
>
> —Matthew 7:34

In Greek mythology, Saturn was dethroned by Jupiter. Nowadays, Saturn is substituted by Uranus, the father of Saturn, who was castrated by his own son. Uranus is unpredictable in nature, producing unforeseeable events.

Saturn rules time. There is no thinking ahead or backwards without Saturn. Saturn is connected with science and everything to do with the future (fate). It does not give a person expectations. (If you expect something, you may be disappointed. Nobody can get everything.)

It is impossible to outsmart Saturn. The wise man will integrate Saturn in his life through time, will power, perseverance, and patience. Time will solve many problems. If a person has such an attitude, Saturn becomes a helper and partner.

With patience a ruler may be persuaded and a soft tongue will break a bone.

—Proverbs of Solomon 25:15

He who is patient like the earth, firm like India's bolt, like a lake free from mud, for him there is no round of births and deaths.

—The Dhammapada: The Sage 6(95)

Saturn is the greatest enemy for a young man, but is a friend for an old man.

A strong Saturn is good for a spiritual approach to life, but bad for one's day-to-day life.

Saturn in Leo harms the Sun, its dispositor. Since Leo rules the heart, Saturn there can cause heart disease.

Perhaps the best position for Saturn is in Pisces, the most evolved of the water signs, the sign of love and compassion.

There is no fear in love, but perfect love casts out fear.

—1 John 4:18

Saturn posited in an angular house or five degrees or less from the cusp of an angular house (the First, the Fourth, the Seventh or the Tenth) is not good because it is too powerful.

Saturn in the Second House may bring tremendous wealth or great poverty.

Saturn in the Fourth House causes unhappiness in childhood and in old age (the beginning and end of life).

If Saturn, the ruler of the Twelfth House in a person's chart, is bodily in the Fourth House, it will become an important influence later in life and may bring wisdom.

Saturn in the Fifth House often shows childlessness, because the drive for procreation is missing.

Saturn in the Seventh House indicates marriage to a Saturnine person, marriage to a significantly older person, a late marriage, or no marriage at all.

Saturn in the Eighth House indicates a slow, progressive sickness and death with suffering, or death from a fall.

Saturn does not incline to much of a belief in God. With Saturn in the Ninth House, a person may be an atheist.

67

Saturn in the Tenth House is not good. It might bring a neurosis; at best, it will bring foresight. If Saturn is in the Tenth House in the birth chart, difficulties will arise whenever Saturn returns to the Tenth House by transit.

And which of you by being anxious can add one cubit to his span of life?

—Matthew 7:27

Saturn in the Eleventh House indicates elderly people as friends.

If Saturn, as ruler of the Fourth House, is in the Twelfth House, it can produce suffering, due to a bad philosophy on the part of the parents. The Twelfth House is the house of misfortunes, and, in relation to cause and effect, it is the Ninth House (knowledge) of the Fourth.

Whatever Saturn destroys, Jupiter rebuilds.

Aspects of Saturn

Saturn in square to the ascendant causes anxiety.

Jupiter in trine to Saturn is a hallmark of entrepreneurs.

The Sun in trine to Saturn will help overcome anxiety and will give foresight.

Saturn in opposition to the Sun is not harmful, if the Sun is above the horizon and Saturn is below.

A conjunction between Saturn and the Moon indicates suppressed instincts. An opposition between Saturn and the Moon is not too bad. The Moon in the Fourth House opposed by Saturn in the Tenth House indicates repression. However, since repression can prove a blessing in disguise, it generally is not too bad an aspect.

Saturn and Mars cannot cooperate. Saturn (postponement) is not good for Mars (immediacy), and Mars is not good for Saturn.

Saturn conjunct Mars is a very dangerous aspect.

Saturn opposed by Mars causes foresight to be postponed.

A square or an opposition between Mars and Saturn is the worst possible aspect. It can harm through violence and anxiety. The aspect will be even worse if either or both of the planets are in dishonour.

An aspect between Uranus and Saturn is difficult in that it brings together two planets with contradictory natures. Uranus symbolizes complete freedom, while Saturn does not want freedom and goes for limitation. In making an interpretation, a lot will depend upon whether these planets aspect the ascendant and/or the mid-heaven, and in what way.

In general, Saturn and Neptune in a bad aspect (square or opposition) will produce an anxiety, which could lead to neurosis, which, in turn, could develop into a psychosis. In particular, a square between Saturn and Neptune will create the anxiety of how to compete in this world.

> It is a strange desire to seek power and to lose liberty or to seek power over others and to lose power over a man's self.
>
> —Francis Bacon

A good aspect between Saturn and Pluto will bring a limitation to Pluto's impetuosity, but much will depend on which is the significator and which is the promissor.

♅ URANUS

Uranus is the general significator of uncommon pursuits, sudden changes of fortune, inventions, discoveries and unconventional relations and actions.

Uranus is stationed in the material sphere, but with a vision of both the material and spiritual spheres.

It is a paradoxical planet, which operates both from above and below, being powerful in mundane things. Along with Mars and Saturn, Uranus is a lord of this world.

It is co-ruler together with Saturn, of Aquarius and the Eleventh House.

Uranus remains seven years in one sign. We do not yet know everything about Uranus, because it emanates new radiations unknown to us. We do not know its values. We do know that Uranus is connected with the parathyroid gland and, according to some astrologers, with the pituitary gland.

The directives of Uranus are unpredictable. Uranus is always changing under the spur of the moment. You cannot foresee events caused by Uranus. Wherever Uranus is, there is a change, a revolution, a search for freedom. Uranus goes against, and takes away, stability.

It is the planet connected with astrology. An astrologer should have a good connection between his Mercury and his Uranus, which will, among other things, cause his thinking to break away from old-fashioned laws. Awareness is the key to change.

Falls and accidents often occur when Uranus transits over one's ascendant.

Uranus is the enemy of the Sun (which represents the will and organization), because in the archetype, Uranus, the ruler of Aquarius, is in opposition to the Sun, the ruler of Leo.

Seldom by itself does Uranus injure the character, but it can create anxiety. It is a disturbing element and has little understanding for psychology.

It is the planet connected with electricity, eccentricity, the unusual.

Uranian knowledge is universal, but does not bring spiritual evolution.

Persons with a strong Saturn and Uranus take advantage of other people. They are the true "users."

Uranus in the First House indicates an unusual person.

If Uranus is in the Fourth House, the native may become a hobo (a wandering, homeless person) around the time he reaches age seventy. This has even happened to wealthy people and to intellectuals.

Uranus shows unusual relationships. Posited in the Fifth House, it often indicates homosexuality.

Uranus is the higher octave of Mercury. If it is in a good aspect with Mercury, it accelerates thinking and everything Mercurial. Too much intelligence, however, might prove dangerous. One must consider "the sanctity of simplicity." A bad aspect between Mercury and Uranus may indicate too much of an acceleration, especially if it is a square.

In an aspect between Uranus and Pluto, Uranus will speed up Pluto, causing restlessness and lack of patience.

In a conjunction between Uranus and the Moon, one should remember that the Moon is easily influenced and that Uranus is always a disturbing element with little understanding for psychology.

According to some astrologers, Uranus is in exaltation in Scorpio, but according to Zoltan S. Mason, Uranus cannot be in honour in the sign belonging to the Eighth House of the archetype, which is the house of death. How can the intelligence of Uranus understand death?

♆ NEPTUNE

Neptune is the planet of the seer, the visionary.

The best of men is the seer.

—The Dhammapada: The Path 1(273)

He who prophesies speaks to men for their upbuilding and encouragement
and consolation.

—1 Corinthians 14:3

It is the planet of inspiration and aspiration, creating high expectations of mankind and of life. It is also the most dangerous of the planets because it does not see reality. It creates illusions and delusions and does not allow one to focus.

Delusion is the bane of humankind.

—The Dhammapada: Craving 25(358)

Neptune is the strongest of the planets during the night, second only to the Moon, which is the strongest of the lights at night.

It is the co-ruler of Pisces, along with Jupiter, and is connected with the Twelfth House.

A very strong Neptune indicates a strongly developed unconscious and a very powerful imagination, but it does not bring good luck, since Neptune, in the archetype, is the co-ruler of the Twelfth House, which is connected with misfortune (mala fortuna).

The quincunx aspect (150 degrees) is Neptunian in nature. It creates indifference, or a retardation resulting from a karmic situation.

Neptune is connected with the pineal gland, through which we communicate with the invisible.

Neptune stays fourteen years in each sign.

The best sign for Neptune to be in is a watery sign, where it is mediumistic. It takes forty-two years for Neptune, once it has left a watery sign, to return to a watery sign.

Neptune is a planet belonging to the mutable (common) cross. It acts to provide the final union of the soul with the spirit. Neptune is always influential in the horoscope of a spiritually evolved person, and, in general, is very important for evolution. It is the planet of "Universal

71

Brotherhood," in which self-preservation gives way to unselfish idealism. Without a strong Neptune, one may not consider the existence of higher forces, but a strong Neptune may cause one to suffer a lot in life.

Neptune sometimes causes an individual to become overly spiritual and to neglect the duties of the physical life altogether, caring neither for health nor for life. Life is a mystery to be experienced and has to be lived.

Wherever Neptune is, there is a secret or an illusion.

Neptune is by nature tremendously sensitive.

Neptune in honour can be too powerful.

Alcohol has a Neptunian influence.

Neptune is the planet ruling toxins, poisons. If one has a strong Neptune, he should avoid alcohol, drugs, smoking, and anything that can produce toxins.

Astrologically, the disease of cancer is caused by a Neptunian intoxication and by a Saturnine lack of elimination of these toxins.

If your Neptune is good, you may dream of future events.

By dwelling on knowledge that presents itself in a dream, steadiness of mind may be procured.

—Patanjali, Book I:39

The best position for a well-aspected Neptune is in the Ninth House where it will work towards metaphysics and higher philosophy. If it is in a watery sign there, it will be very influential. It will produce the qualities of a mystic.

It is sometimes very difficult to bring out one's true nature and abilities. The pupil and the teacher must be one within the same person. The teacher arrives when the pupil is ready (i.e., when the pupil is prepared to attune himself with his higher self).

Just as with the other modern planets, Neptune is important for persons who are innovative.

Neptune is the higher octave of Venus. As such, Neptune signifies physical and spiritual love as distinct from the solely physical love of Venus.

He who does not love does not know God, for God is love.

—1 John 4:8

Neptune represents compassion; it does not discriminate. It is much more evolved than Venus. It gives freedom to the emotions and is connected with the sex drive.

If Venus is in a good zodiacal state, Neptune can develop the third eye (also called the seventh sense) which is needed by an astrologer, so that he can feel how a person receives the planetary influences, and so that he can study the human soul.

An astrologer should have a powerful Neptune, which will provide him with inspiration. A powerful Neptune should be able to be detected from the hand of a person. Incidentally, the deeper the lines in the hand of a person, the more substance the person's life has.

A strongly Neptunian person will pick up the vibrations of others, whether good or bad. That is why the Neptunian influence is so dangerous. Neptune is especially bad when it is in an opposition or a square with Saturn (the guardian of the threshold).

Neptune in the Fifth House could produce an unrealistic view of, and strange approach to, love.

If Neptune is in a person's Seventh House, the human environment of the person, i.e., his partners, will not be rational.

As co-ruler of the Twelfth House of the Zodiac, Neptune will be outstanding in the chart of people working in jails, hospitals, etc.

Neptune posited in the Twelfth House, although a cadent house, can be too influential, due to its being the natural ruler of this house. Karmic debt is in the Twelfth House: "We have to pay for previous debts."

All aspects of Neptune will cause exaggerated imagination.

A conjunction between the Moon and Neptune could prove very dangerous, in that it will make it difficult to experience reality.

Neptune well-aspected by other planets gives fantasy.

A square between the Moon and Neptune reflects a lack of clear sight—there will be too much fantasy.

♇ PLUTO

Pluto is the co-ruler, together with Mars, of the eighth sign of the Zodiac (Scorpio). It rules what is hidden, yet active. It reflects the impact and the pressure of the unconscious on the conscious.

The astrologer Charles Vougas, whose speciality was Pluto, wrote:

Pluto reveals what still lies in part of the self to be conquered through a second descent towards a previous stage of its evolution, thus leading the self to darkness and yet unexplored levels of its nature, the domain of primitive man within ourselves that has to be explored and still conceals itself under the veneer of social prerequisites.

Pluto reflects the servitudes of a person's past and haunts the depth of the unconscious.

Pluto is very destructive and divisive. It disintegrates and its force is centrifugal.

Kruger (the Swedish tycoon of the 1920s) had Pluto in the Tenth House, and Marilyn Monroe had it in the First House.

Pluto will always cause a retardation. "You get too soon old and too late smart." Pluto destroys with the idea to rebuild something better, but usually this cannot be achieved, because of lack of time.

Pluto has two markedly opposite qualities. It is connected with the gangster and racketeer when its destructive side manifests, and with the highest type of spiritual effort and realization of cosmic work by an individual, when its better side is manifested.

Blessed are the peacemakers, for they shall be called sons of God.

—Matthew 5:9

Pluto in Scorpio will provoke excess. In consequence, the present times are most destructive, due to the influence of Pluto in Scorpio, which reached its peak in 1989, when Pluto was in the middle of the sign (15 degrees of Scorpio). During the time that Pluto is in Scorpio, people will need even greater fortitude in facing the trials of life. The best approach is to provide a good example to others. One must work against the destructive influences of Pluto in Scorpio with perseverance and by using one's will.

The intelligent man, represented by Mercury, will not accept such destructive influences because Mercury is peregrine in Scorpio. The wise man, represented by Jupiter, will react in a different way because Jupiter, being in honour of triplicity in Scorpio, represents wisdom. Such a man will direct his intelligence towards finding a solution to the problems.

Jupiter in Scorpio will cooperate with Pisces and with Cancer (which stands for security and in which Jupiter is exalted).

One who cannot find harmony in himself must look to the opposite sign for help. This would be another approach to facing Pluto in Scorpio. Venus (ruler of Taurus, the sign opposite Scorpio) and the Moon (ruler of Taurus by exaltation) should be emphasized and become influential.

From the position and the aspects of Pluto, we can get an indication of how much the deep nature of a human being can change.

Finally, be strong in the Lord and in the strength of his might. Put on the whole armour of God, that you may be able to stand against the wiles of the devil. For we are not contending against flesh and blood, but against principalities, against the powers, against the world rulers of this present darkness, against the spiritual hosts of wickedness in the heavenly places. Therefore take the whole armour of God, that you may be able to withstand in the evil day, and having done all to stand. Stand therefore having girded your loins, with truth, and having put on the breastplate of righteousness, and having shod your feet with the equipment of the gospel of peace; above all taking the shield of faith, with which you can quench all the flaming darts of the evil one. And take the helmet of salvation, and the sword of the Spirit, which is the word of God. Pray at all times in the Spirit, with all prayer and supplication.

—Ephesians 6:10–18

The Signs

When you are able to interpret completely the twelve signs of the zodiac, you will know astrology.

Truth has twelve faces. If you are spiritually evolved, no sign will harm you. "Live and let live." A sign is judged by its ruler and is expressed by the way in which the planetary influences coming from it are received. Each sign is 30 degrees. A sign's influence will not be very strong in the first three degrees or in the last three degrees.

Happiness comes from a benefic rising sign (ascendant).

Each sign is a pictograph, which gives a lot of information. For example, Pisces is symbolized by two fish. Defenseless, they swim in opposite directions. In this sign, consciousness is missing. That is why the Twelfth House, which is associated with Pisces in the archetype, is the house of sleep, where there is no consciousness.

> Sleep is that qualification of the mind which ensues upon the quitting of all objects of the mind, by reason of all the weakening senses and faculties sinking into abeyance.
>
> —Patanjali, Book I:10

> We are such stuff as dreams are made on, and our little life is rounded with a sleep.
>
> —*The Tempest*, IV.i, Shakespeare

Opposite signs work together. A sign learns from its opposite. What a sign does not have in itself, it may try to gain through overcompensation. Each sign has two other signs of the same triplicity with which it must cooperate. Thus, one should never think only of one sign. One must think of the entire triplicity.

Each sign is the domicile of a planet.

The Jupiterian signs are: Sagittarius, Pisces,
Cancer (by exaltation)

The Saturnine signs are: Aquarius, Capricorn,
Libra (by exaltation)

The Venusian signs are:	Taurus, Libra, Pisces (by exaltation)
The Martian signs are:	Aries, Scorpio, Capricorn (by exaltation)
The Mercurial signs are:	Gemini, Virgo (by domicile and by exaltation)

It is not good for the King (the Sun) or the Queen (the Moon) to be in a sign ruled by Mercury, such as Virgo, and in the House of the Servant (the sixth house in the archetype), and therefore in no aspect with the rising sign, even though the King and Queen need the servant (Mercury likes to serve).

Gemini, Leo, and Virgo are considered to be barren, celibate signs.

The signs on the cusps of the Second, Third, and Fourth Houses are influential during the last part of a person's life.

An intercepted sign is weaker than one that is not, because it is as if the sign were imprisoned. Therefore, it follows that a planet in an intercepted sign is less influential than one that is not. However, there are some astrologers—Alan Leo, for example—who believe the opposite to be true.

The shortcomings of an intercepted sign can be ameliorated by overcompensation or by changing one's location (moving to a different place on the earth).

Whenever there is more than one planet in a sign, the most influential will be the one in domicile. If none is in domicile, then the most influential will be the one in exaltation. If none is in honour, then the one nearest to the cusp of the sign will be the most influential.

Distortion

A distortion occurs when there is an intercepted sign, or when the signs belonging to the triplicity of the rising sign are missing from the cusps of either or both the Fifth and Ninth Houses. While distortions can occur in horoscopes, in the archetypal zodiac in the sky there are never distortions.

A distortion is not desirable; the ideal horoscope is not distorted. Those people born on or near the equator do not have distorted horoscopes. The closer one is born to the poles, the more likely the horoscope will be distorted.

A person will have normal, healthy outlets if his horoscope is free of intercepted signs.

One's element is that of his rising sign. If the same element of matter (earth, water, air, or fire) is not also on the Fifth and Ninth House cusps, one will have a lack of understanding for the affairs of those houses.

In order to evolve, a human being needs two outlets: love and higher knowledge (the Fifth and the Ninth Houses). The purpose of the incarnation of a soul is to evolve through experiences by being connected with other souls on the material plane (the earth).

The Fifth House (house of love, pleasure, children, and hobbies) is a good house. It is the realization of the Eighth House (house of regeneration). If there is a distortion between the First and the Fifth Houses through a square aspect, the native's love will go towards his home or his work. These will become his outlets. However, the square aspect will cause him to struggle or fight, and to force the issues with regard to his love life. The difficulty here is that since love belongs to the unconscious, the issues really cannot be forced. You cannot struggle to have love or to give love to another person. You cannot force the issues for pleasure, children, or hobbies either.

Generally, a person who is unhappy, owing to his Fifth House, will compensate by becoming very involved with his profession, which then becomes the pleasure or hobby.

Hope deferred makes the heart sick, but a desire fulfilled is a tree of life.

—Proverbs 13:12

If there is a distortion between the First and Fifth Houses through a quincunx aspect, there will be no love or struggle for it, and there may be no children, or at least no great understanding for them. With a quincunx aspect, or with no aspect at all, the person will neglect the issues. The love will tend towards purely physical love. There will be no communication on the emotional level, since the "love" will be irrational and unyielding to conditions.

In the case of a quincunx aspect between the First House and the Fifth House, the person will usually accept his lot or become a philosopher.

It is not good to accept your lot, but it is good to improve it.

—Anonymous

When there is a distortion between the First and the Ninth Houses, there will be an inability to have a relationship with God and higher knowledge. With such a distortion, a person might go to church, but will be unable to experience God.

The farther North one is born, the more distorted the horoscope becomes, and the more a person will be unable to understand life in a harmonious way. People born near the equator are simpler in their approach to life.

The most important thing is the survival of the person, and second, the survival of the race.

The Seal of Solomon

The Seal of Solomon can be interpreted as a six-pointed star formed of two interlocking equilateral triangles, one of which connects the First, Fifth, and Ninth House cusps, and the other of which connects the Seventh, Eleventh, and Third House cusps. Assuming there are no distortions, each triangle connects three signs of the same triplicity. The triplicity formed by the First, Fifth, and Ninth Houses is connected with the native, and that formed by the Third, Seventh, and Eleventh Houses is connected with his partners.

Male and Female Signs

The spirit is masculine, and the soul is feminine. The sex of a sign determines whether it is active or reactive.

Male signs are active, extroverted, connected with the Sun (the conscious, the will-power) and inspire female signs. Male signs are connected with the odd-numbered houses, 1, 3, 5, 7, 9, and 11 in the archetype. Usually, a male sign incites one to make a decision (although sometimes too soon). Don't look for understanding of the human soul, or of the dream world, in a male sign. A soldier must have the majority of planets in male signs. Male signs positioned above the horizon will be strong and more extroverted than those positioned below the horizon. This is because the area above the horizon is ruled by the Sun, while the area below the horizon is ruled by the Moon, which is feminine.

Female signs, connected with the even numbered houses 2, 4, 6, 8, 10, and 12, are reactive and connected with the Moon (impressions and the unconscious). Female signs are the night domiciles of their rulers. Female signs are responsive, and tend to be indecisive, but it is better to make a wrong decision than no decision; it is better to fail than not to struggle.

If a man has many planets in feminine signs, or a woman has many planets in male signs, there is the tendency toward bisexuality, which could be reflected in the choice of the profession.

With the majority of planets in female signs, a man could also be tremendously attracted to women (see Robert Kennedy's birth chart).

Triplicities

The triplicities are connected with the four elements of matter (earth, water, air, and fire). The difference between each triplicity is seen in the extent to which the atoms are heated or cooled. For courage, the atoms must be heated. Courage belongs to the conscious. You can acquire it through volition.

The quantity of an element may distort the harmony of a horoscope.

Earth wants to work. It is cold and dry and is associated with winter.

Water wants to love. It is cold and wet and is associated with autumn.

Air wants to communicate. It is hot and wet and is associated with spring.

Fire wants to dominate. It is hot and dry and is associated with summer.

Earth

Earth is the most solid manifestation of matter. It is connected with the material plane and the mineral kingdom, and shows the greatest resistance. Earth is connected with self-preservation and survival. People with a lot of earth signs in their horoscopes are often melancholic and pessimistic. These people may imagine that money buys everything. Money and all physical possessions come from the earth. "Come down to earth!" is a popular phrase. Earth, in a general way, is connected with financial security, and has no sensitivity. Earth does not spend money; it wants to make it. Earth does not love. It has great foresight, but it is not wise.

Taurus, Virgo, and Capricorn are the signs of the earth. With the ascendant in an earthy sign, the constitution is strong.

Earth is connected with the planet Saturn, the ruler of the Tenth House (Capricorn) in the archetype. Saturn represents old age and senility.

Earth needs water (humidity—emotions).

On the spiritual level, an earthy person will be attracted to fire. However, he will be inclined to annihilate fire's enthusiasm.

Water

Water is more evolved than earth. Water belongs to the vegetal kingdom (flora) and to the astral plane. It is connected with the desires, the emotions, and the instincts. Water is less resistant than earth. The three water signs are Cancer, Scorpio, and Pisces. Water needs earth even though it is exploited by it. Because water always follows a downward course, evolution is achieved through sustained inspiration and unfailing will power. Water is found in plenty in the human being. Fifty percent of the physical body is water. The lack of water in the human being can be due to Saturn, which rules the skin (outer structure) and the bones (inner structure). Saturn can reduce the amount of water in the body.

In early astrology books, water was never explained because it is connected with the unconscious, and is, therefore, secretive. Love and procreation belong to water; it symbolizes the giver, the sperm. The result of the emotions is a family. The emotions are completely dependent on the unconscious and are not connected with intelligence. Intelligence and love do not go together. You have to be emotional at home and cold in your profession. The emotions take away the drive of the water signs. Whatever has to do with emotions represents difficulties. Emotional problems are so individual that they can hardly be solved. Without water in one's horoscope, one cannot understand human beings. Without water, there is no pity, no understanding.

And the Spirit of God was moving over the face of the waters.

—Genesis 1:2

The Myth of Vishnou

These myths help us to understand the mystery of another, hidden element, the sacred power of Vishnou. The sea, the rain, the blood, the sperm or milk, it is always a substance endowed with the potentiality of change and transmutation. When Narada asks to be taught its secret, Vishnou does not give him an answer but speaks of the water as a straight thoroughfare that is of initiation because initiation always denotes a passage from one point to another, from the visible to the invisible and from one state into another, from the manifest to its opposite. On the hidden plan to be emerged in, the water signifies the search for and the perception of the mystery of life.

—Hades: Manuel complet d'Astrologie Mondiale, Editions Niclaus

Then went out to him Jerusalem and all Judea and all the region about the Jordan, and they were baptized by Him in the river Jordan, confessing their sins.

—Matthew 3:5

In those days Jesus came from Nazareth of Galilee and was baptized by John in the Jordan. And when he came out of the water, immediately he saw the heavens opened and the spirit descending upon him like a dove.

—Mark 1:9,10

Air

Air belongs to the animal kingdom and the lower mental plane. It is connected with intelligence and communication, the purpose of which is to increase understanding. Without air, no communication would be possible.

Air is the triplicity of truth. It needs fire for realization. Air, boundless and expanding by nature, lacks a centre. It is not selfish.

Gemini, Libra, and Aquarius are the three air signs.

If the majority of the planets in a horoscope are in airy signs, the native may be tall.

Fire

Fire belongs to the human kingdom and the higher mental plane. In the Zodiac, fire represents Heaven. Fire needs air for its realization. The enthusiasm of fire cannot exist without air (communication). A leader must be a good communicator.

Aries, Leo, Sagittarius are the three fire signs.

Fire signs give motivation and enthusiasm for activity. Many planets in fire signs will give tremendous enthusiasm and the possibility for leadership.

The fiery person will never have an inferiority complex. Fire does not know anxiety.

Fire is connected with action, volition, and consciousness. Fire represents the true evolution of the human being. It is inclined to stay away from the earth and earthly values; earth extinguishes fire. The divine unity in the Rosicrucian Fire is symbolic of fire.

As was the man of dust, so are those who are of dust, and as is the man of heaven, so are those who are of heaven. Just as we have borne the image of the man of dust, we shall also bear the image of the man of heaven.

—1 Corinthians 15:48,49

A fire sign on the ascendant will give a good constitution.

Quadruplicities

The quadruplicities can be thought of in terms of the centrifugal and centripetal force of atoms. The atoms of the cardinal signs move in a centrifugal fashion. The atoms of the fixed signs never change, revolving around a centre point in a centripetal fashion, and the atoms of the mutable signs always change, their atoms moving back and forth like a pendulum.

Cardinal signs are Aries, Cancer, Libra, and Capricorn, associated in the archetype with Houses 1, 4, 7, and 10 respectively. They show a direction, a purpose, a goal, which they pursue to the end. Cardinal signs give fortitude. A cardinal sign makes a decision right away and always moves ahead in one direction. This is an indication of an evolved person.

Cardinal signs are twice as strong as fixed signs, and four times as strong as common-mutable signs. If someone has a cardinal sign rising, don't expect pity from him.

The cardinal cross provides great drive and will power. Only with a cardinal cross can you change your relationship with your parents and obtain high spiritual evolution, but it is not connected with happiness.

The fixed signs are Taurus, Leo, Scorpio, and Aquarius, associated in the archetype with Houses 2, 5, 8, and 11 respectively. The Sphinx in Egypt represents the fixed signs and the passage of time. With a fixed sign, there is no change. The attitude of a fixed sign is "If it was good for my father, it will be good for me, and it will be good for my son also." The centre of a fixed sign is the person himself. If a person with a fixed sign rising falls in love with you, he or she will not change—the love will be permanent.

A fixed sign is only 50 percent as strong as a cardinal sign. With a fixed cross, one's relationship with one's parents cannot be changed.

The common-mutable signs are Gemini, Virgo, Sagittarius, and Pisces (the two Mercurial and the two Jupiterian signs) associated with Houses 3, 6, 9, and 12 respectively. Double-bodied signs are always mutable. The nature of mutable signs is primarily mental. They are adaptable and can therefore adjust easily. The mutability of a sign is seen in its lack of direction and in its lack of motivation. Mutable signs can see both sides as a process of their intelligence or wisdom. Intelligence is connected with air and earth (Mercury), and wisdom with water and fire (Jupiter). Intelligence will realize itself in wisdom. According to Patanjali (the Indian Yogi of the second century A.D.), wisdom is that knowledge which is absolutely free from error.

The attitude of a mutable sign is "I am tired of the status quo. I want a change." A mutable sign does not stick to things. Mutability does not promote strength; it is not an asset when trying to develop one's will power. With a mutable sign, there is a continuous change. Mutable signs are only 25 percent as strong as cardinal signs and 50 percent as strong as fixed signs.

Air reflects truth and understanding.

Human and Animal Signs

The signs can be divided also into human and animal signs. The human signs are good for humanitarian goals.

The human signs are Gemini, Virgo, Libra, and Aquarius.

The animal signs are Aries, Taurus, Cancer, Leo, Scorpio, Capricorn, and Pisces.

Sagittarius is half-human (the first 15 degrees of the sign) and half-animal (the last 15 degrees of the sign).

The Twelve Signs of the Zodiac

♈ ARIES

Aries is the first sign of the zodiac. It is the cardinal sign of the fire triplicity, and it is dry and hot. The ruler of the sign is Mars, which is the natural ruler of the First House. The Sun is the ruler of Aries through exaltation. The Sun there indicates attraction to a spiritual approach and is good for leadership, especially if it is in the Tenth House. With the Sun in Aries, a person will have a direction towards others, away from himself. He will not derive power from himself, but from the others. However, the Sun in Aries can give arrogance.

Venus is in detriment in Aries, and Saturn is in fall there. Jupiter is in honour of triplicity, and the Moon and Mercury are peregrine.

A man with Aries rising will be the ideal for a woman, but he may have an ego problem.

For Aries to be of a good quality in a horoscope, Pisces must be good.

The Moon in Aries gives a tremendous drive because of Mars, the ruler of the sign.

Aries does not know pity.

We need the idealism of Aries.

♉ TAURUS

Taurus is the second sign of the zodiac. It is the sign on the cusp of the Second House in the archetype. Taurus is the night domicile of Venus, its natural ruler. The Moon rules Taurus by exaltation. Mars is in detriment in Taurus. Saturn and Mercury are in honour of triplicity, and the Sun and Jupiter are peregrine there. Taurus represents the sex sign of women. (Scorpio is the sex sign of men.) A woman with the Sun or the ascendant in Taurus may be especially appealing to men.

A person with his or her ascendant in Taurus will have a strong connection with the physical world and with money.

The sign of Taurus is connected with work. The Taurean personality will work lifelong. Taurus, because it is a fixed sign, likes stability and security; it dislikes uncertainty and change. This is the reason why Uranus, the planet of instability, sudden decision, and disorganization, would not be in a good zodiacal state in Taurus.

Better is a little with righteousness than great revenue with injustice.

—Proverbs 16:13

Wealth hastily gotten will dwindle but he who gathers little by little will increase it.

—Proverbs 13:11

⛎ GEMINI

Gemini corresponds to the third sign of the zodiac and the Third House in the archetype. It is a mutable, human sign ruled by the planet Mercury, and is situated, by its position, on the cusp of the Third House, below the horizon in the archetype. Neither of the lights (Sun or Moon) is in honour in Gemini. The values of Gemini are very superficial. It is the sign of greatest duality of the zodiac. Gemini typifies the quality that sustains all worlds, that alone makes life and consciousness possible.

In Gemini, Jupiter is in detriment, Venus and Saturn are in honour of triplicity, and the Sun, Moon, and Mars are peregrine. Mercury, the planet of mental expression, is in domicile in Gemini. Jupiter is weak in a Mercurial sign, while Mercury is weak in a Jupiterian sign.

The person with a strong Gemini changes constantly. He thinks too much. A good mind does not necessarily bring happiness.

Gemini in the Third House indicates intellectual curiosity and an inclination to read many books at the same time.

The Second House (the house of money) is the secret enemy of the Third House (the house of intelligence). Intelligence is based on foresight. Intelligence will realize itself in wisdom.

Keep your life free from love of money, and be content with what you have: for he has said, "I will never fail you or forsake you."
—Hebrews 13:5

To get wisdom is better than gold, to get understanding is to be chosen rather than silver.

—Proverbs 16:16

He who loves money will not be satisfied with money: nor he who loves wealth, with pain: this also is vanity.

—Ecclesiastes 5:10

Gemini on the ascendant shows the desire for complete freedom on both the intellectual and material planes.

Mercury, the ruler of Gemini, shows, according to whether it is in a cardinal, fixed or mutable sign, if the desires of the native will be of any value. The native will have a youthful attitude and will be interested in, and involved in, many things at the same time. He will learn by communication: by talking and listening to others, etc. However, his knowledge will be superficial.

♋ CANCER

The sign of Cancer corresponds to the fourth sign of the zodiac and to the Fourth House in the archetype. It is the cardinal sign of the water triplicity. With the Moon its ruler, it is humid and cold. Cancer is connected with pity, due to Jupiter being exalted there.

A wise son makes a good father, but a foolish man despises his mother.

—Proverbs 15:20

A fool despises his father's instruction but he who heeds admonition is prudent.

—Proverbs 15:5

If cosmic waters are the originator of everything they are also their tomb. There is a consistence thereof. The sign of Cancer, cardinal sign of the water element, corresponds to the ocean, to the beginning of life, but also to the Fourth House in its capacity as the fourth sign of the Zodiac. One of the attributions of the Fourth House is indeed the tomb as well as the "end of things." The water always follows a downward course and goes to the bottom; this is the cause of the supernatural properties attributed to its signs.

—Hades: Manuel complet d'Astrologie
Mondiale, Editions Niclaus

According to Zoltan Mason, the three signs of the water triplicity may be depicted as follows: Cancer as a running stream or river, Scorpio as a stagnant pool, and Pisces as an ocean.

Mercury and Venus are peregrine in Cancer. The Sun is also peregrine in Cancer but brings luck there. Jupiter is exalted in Cancer, and so it is considered a beneficial sign and a sign of wisdom. Saturn in Cancer is in detriment and can indicate danger for the mother of the native. Mars in Cancer is in fall and can indicate mistakes made because of emotions.

Cancer on the ascendant gives tremendous sensitivity.

♌ LEO

Leo, a fixed sign, corresponds to the fifth sign of the zodiac, and to the Fifth House in the archetype. It is ruled by the Sun.

Leo is the sign associated with kings and with greatness. It is a charismatic sign and the sign of volition. Leo has a very strong desire to rule others, but, generally, does not want to take responsibilities.

For the upright will inhabit the land and the treacherous will be rooted out.

—Proverbs 2:21

The animal associated with Leo is the lion. It is a dangerous animal, but does not attack unless it is hungry.

According to some astrologers, the sign of Leo is the most masculine of the signs.

Leo has no pity. (The moment one has pity, he cannot achieve his goals.) However, people with Leo on the ascendant like to give to others, but when it comes to love, they love only themselves. Leo is ego-centered.

The sign of Leo does not want to work. It rules the Fifth House, which is the house of love, pleasures, and hobbies. Leo wants to enjoy life.

In Leo, Mars and Jupiter are in honour of triplicity. Saturn is in detriment, and Mercury, Venus, and the Moon are peregrine.

The person who has Leo on his ascendant will have a strong will and will want to be the king.

If such a person has little or no will, we must look for an interference in the horoscope. In order to exercise the volition (Leo), one has to overcome his emotions (Cancer), since emotions take away drive.

Leo has no foresight. (Foresight is connected only with the earth signs.)

Be not wise in your own eyes: fear the Lord, and turn away from evil. It will be healing to your flesh and refreshment to your bones.

—Proverbs 2:7,8

No ill befalls the righteous but the wicked are filled with trouble.

—Proverbs 12:21

Leo in the Eleventh House will indicate very influential friends.

A person with Leo on his ascendant will make money if the next sign, Virgo, an earth sign, is on his Second House cusp. Leo personalities must cultivate courage (Aries) and wisdom (Sagittarius).

♍ VIRGO

Virgo is the sixth sign of the zodiac, connected with the Sixth House in the archetype. It is a human and mutable sign ruled by Mercury, which is not only in domicile, but is also exalted there. Virgo is the night domicile of Mercury. Virgo can analyze, but not synthesize.

The sign of Virgo is good for an intelligent person, but is not good for a person who is at a low level of evolution. For such a person, exaltation is worthless.

Virgo shows an interest in money because it is an earthy sign, not because it is ruled by Mercury, which is simply an agent, and, in this sign, a business agent.

The sign of Leo is the secret enemy of Virgo.

Virgo is the sign associated with service to others. The Virgo personality needs to be self-assertive; if not, there is great unhappiness. Although they are inquisitive by nature, Virgo subjects tend to avoid asking questions. (They feel that it might undermine their self-assertion.)

In Virgo, Jupiter is in detriment, Venus is in fall, Saturn is in honour of triplicity, and the Sun, the Moon, and Mars are peregrine.

Virgo as a rising sign is excellent for the service professions: nursing, medicine, etc., as well as for work requiring detail and precision.

Find Happiness in Service

In all things I must have shown you that by so toiling, one must help the weak, remembering the words of Lord Jesus, how he said, "It is more blessed to give than to receive."

—Acts 20:35

 # LIBRA

A false balance is an abomination to the Lord, but a just weight is his delight.

—Proverbs 11:1

A just balance and scales are the Lord's; all the weights in the bag are his work.

—Proverbs 16:11

Libra is a cardinal sign, corresponding to the seventh sign of the zodiac and the Seventh House in the archetype. It is connected with partnerships of all types (marriage as well as business), open enemies, lawsuits, and the public.

Venus is the ruler of Libra.

The symbol for Libra represents the Sun rising at daybreak as well as the Sun setting in the evening; thus, it represents the time that divides day from night.

Libra is connected with harmony, peace, fairness, the sense of coordination, and aesthetics in general.

Libra can look backwards six signs to the past and forwards six signs to the future. It is the two-faced Janus of the Romans. It is a sign more connected with human beings than with animals.

Libra is the most evolved of the signs, with Venus in domicile, Saturn in exaltation, and Mercury in honour of triplicity, indicating tremendous intelligence. In Libra, Mars is in detriment, the Sun is in fall, and the Moon and Jupiter are peregrine.

For the Libra personality, the environment is very important because Libra (an air sign) wants to communicate. If the ruler of the sign, Venus, is good (in a good zodiacal state or receives good aspects), communication with others will be pleasant.

Libra is the ideal rising sign for a woman; through Venus (in its day domicile there) she has beauty, through Saturn (exalted there) she has seriousness and foresight, and through Mercury (in honour of triplicity there) she has intelligence.

He who finds a wife finds a good thing, and obtains favour from the Lord.

—Proverbs 18:12

The sign of Libra expresses an equilibrium between the Venusian enjoyment of life and the Saturnine seriousness of life.

♏ SCORPIO

Scorpio is the eighth sign of the zodiac, which corresponds to the Eighth House in the archetype. It is a fixed sign and is connected with death, reincarnation, spiritual communion, legacies, partner's money, and the sex drive.

Scorpio is a beastly sign. It is a strong sign, but its strength is an inner strength, silent in nature.

Weapons and espionage are both connected with Scorpio. Scorpio is the general significator of fruitfulness. On the ascendant, it gives a strong sex drive, as well as the ability to understand the problems of life and death.

The sex sign belonging to a man is Scorpio. (That belonging to a woman is Taurus.)

The rulers of Scorpio are Mars and Pluto. Mars is in its night domicile in Scorpio.

In Scorpio, Jupiter is in honour of triplicity, Venus is in detriment, Mercury, Saturn, and the Sun are peregrine, and the Moon is in fall.

Scorpio is the sign opposite Taurus, where Venus is the ruler and the Moon is in exaltation. A sign must work together with its opposite. Venus and the Moon counterbalance Scorpio, but the Moon in Scorpio, being in fall, shows perversion (example: Henry Miller's birth chart). It can cause an exaggerated sex drive, which might lead to rape. Scorpio is emotional because it is a water sign, but the emotions are hidden and are primarily connected with sex.

Scorpio is violent through Mars. (Charles Manson had four planets [a stellium] in Scorpio.)

The secret enemy of Scorpio is Libra, the sign of marriage. (A sign's secret enemy is always the preceding sign.)

Scorpio can achieve wisdom by transforming material or physical desires into spiritual aspiration (example: Rudolf Steiner's birth chart).

> Riches do not profit in the day of wrath, but righteousness delivers from death.

> —Proverbs 11:4

> Know that wisdom is such to your soul; if you find it, there will be a future, and your hope will not be cut off.

> —Proverbs 24:14

Through transcendence, one can get away from matter and divert a multitude of desires to a higher purpose. The symbol of this is the eagle. Scorpio can also sink into the pleasure of the senses. In such cases, Scorpio is represented by a second symbol, the snake, which stands for matter and material life.

"When the snake burns away the Phoenix comes out." Everyone should try to rise above his lower Scorpio nature and aspire to wisdom, his higher nature, symbolized by the Phoenix.

Is it not true that one must die in a sense on one level, in order to reach a higher level?

Sagittarius, the sign following Scorpio, is ruled by Jupiter, and reflects the highest level of spirit, of faith, and of communication with the world above.

Through the transmutation of Scorpio, one reaches Sagittarius, the ninth sign, the last number of the Master. If a person can overcome the material plane, i.e., human passions, and reach for higher knowledge, he will be able to reach the mid-heaven or the tenth sign, Capricorn, which is the apex of the triangle, the top of the seal of Solomon.

The main characteristic of Scorpio is the struggle between the snake and the eagle:

> Now the works of the flesh are plain: immorality, impurity, licentiousness, idolatry, sorcery, emnity, strife, envy, drunkenness, carousing, and the like. I warn you as I warned you before, that those who do such things shall not inherit the Kingdom of God.

—Galatians 5:19–21

> But in the fruit of the Spirit is love, joy, peace, patience, kindness, goodness, faithfulness, gentleness, self-control; against such things there is no law and those who belong to Christ Jesus have crucified the flesh with its passions and desires.

—Galatians 5:22–24

↗ SAGITTARIUS

Sagittarius is a mutable, half-human, and half-animal sign. The first 15 degrees of the sign are human in nature; the second 15 degrees are animal in nature. Sagittarius likes change for the sake of change. It is energetic, impulsive, and action-oriented.

Sagittarius, being ruled by Jupiter, is the sign of wisdom. In Sagittarius, Mercury is in detriment, Mars and the Sun are in honour of triplicity, and the Moon, Venus, and Saturn peregrine.

Sagittarius on the ascendant gives humanistic qualities: the native will be connected with other people and will always be working to improve himself.

Sagittarius is the ninth sign of the Zodiac, corresponding to the Ninth House in the archetype, and is connected with philosophy and long journeys.

> Trust in the Lord with all your heart, and do not rely on your own insight. In all your ways acknowledge Him and He will make straight your paths.

—Proverbs 3:5,6

A good Sagittarius brings advantages to Capricorn.
Too many planets in Sagittarius create confusion.

♑ CAPRICORN

Capricorn, the tenth sign in the zodiac and the cardinal sign of the earth triplicity, is dry and cold. It is a double-bodied sign in that it is half-terrestrial, and half-fish, meaning it can survive both on earth and in water.

Capricorn is very practical. It is connected with survival. The urge to stay alive (survive) is a healthy instinct. In order to survive, one often must follow necessity (Saturn) and not his own nature.

The unprepared will not survive in life. One should "Pray and work" (Ora et labora).

> Faith firmly rooted is happiness.
>
> —The Dhammapada: The Elephant 14(333)

Capricorn is the most earthy sign of the Zodiac. It expresses an equilibrium that will result in crystallization. Crystallization reflects purity.

Capricorn is associated with poverty or economy. It is receptive and reflective, because it is a feminine sign. Its subjects tend to listen rather than to talk.

Capricorn subjects are inclined to be lonely persons, because Saturn, the ruler of Capricorn, isolates.

Capricorn inhibits through Saturn, but a strong Saturn in Capricorn can be good for a spiritual approach.

> The Lord is a stronghold to him whose way is upright.
>
> —Proverbs 10:29

A spiritual approach implies the ascension towards the sky (Heaven), the world of higher knowledge. Moses received the Book of the Covenant, in communion with God, on the top of Mount Sinai:

> The people cannot come up to Mount Sinai: for thou thyself didst charge us saying "Set bounds about the mountain and consecrate it."
>
> —Exodus 19:23

Similarly, in the New Testament, Jesus said:

Straight is the gate, and narrow is the way, which leadeth unto life, and few there be that find it.

—Matthew 7:14

However, because the ruler of Capricorn, Saturn, is an earthy planet, it is often very bad in that it makes the flow of atoms near the earth to be too heavy. A strong Saturn in Capricorn can cause a neurosis. The only outlet for too strong a Saturn, other than a spiritual approach, is to use one's anxiety for one's own profit.

Anxiety in a man's heart weighs him down, but a good word makes him glad.

—Proverbs 12:25

On the human level, the sign of Capricorn is connected with the Tenth House in the archetype (the highest of all the houses), which corresponds to authority, and the realization and achievements of the individual.

Mars is exalted in Capricorn, indicating that there cannot be wisdom without activity.

Separate not thyself from the congregation.

—Hillel

The Moon is in detriment in Capricorn. Whenever the Moon is in Capricorn, there is anxiety and the inclination to make money (a money-oriented approach to life). Jupiter is in fall in Capricorn, Mercury and Venus are in honour of triplicity, and the Sun is peregrine there.

With Capricorn on the ascendant, the native, even though he may be yet a child, is already old.

Aquarius brings a gain to Capricorn. Aquarius cannot develop without a good Capricorn.

Capricorn in the Third House (house of learning) signifies very serious studies because the ruler of the sign, Saturn, stands for seriousness.

♒ AQUARIUS

Aquarius is a fixed sign corresponding to the Eleventh House in the archetype. It is a human, air sign.

Astrologically, Aquarius represents the highest form of intelligence. The Aquarian intellect creates new inventions every day.

The symbol of Aquarius is two wavy lines. These lines represent air and the desires, which are in equilibrium as a result of knowledge of both good and evil, thus reflecting true wisdom.

> They who discern evil as evil and what is not evil as not evil enter the good path, following the true doctrine.
>
> —The Dhammapada: The Downward Path 14(319)

Aquarius is the general significator of friends, associates, hopes, and wishes.

Saturn, co-ruler with Uranus of Aquarius, is less dangerous in Aquarius than in Capricorn, since the flow of atoms is less heavy in the air than on the earth. In Aquarius, the Sun is in detriment, Mercury and Venus are in honour of triplicity, and the Moon, Mars, and Jupiter are peregrine.

Aquarius cannot develop without a good Capricorn.

In the coming two thousand years, called the Aquarian Age or the New Age, we shall be influenced by the rulers and transmitters of Aquarius: Saturn and Uranus. Saturn will cause pessimism, and Uranus will cause instability. The Aquarian Age will produce a tremendous increase in technology.

In the archetype, the co-ruler of the sign, Uranus, is in trine with its underlying planet, Mercury, ruler of the Third House, Gemini (technology).

Aquarians tend not to live in the present. Some people by their attitude in life are already living in the Aquarian Age, and some others are still far from it.

Time of Stress

> But understand this, that in the last days there will come times of stress. For men will be lovers of self, lovers of money, proud, arrogant, allusive, disobedient to their parents, ungrateful, unholy, impatient, implacable,

slanderous, profligates, fierce, haters of good, treacherous, reckless, swollen with conceit, lovers of pleasure than lovers of God, holding the form of religion but defying the power of it. Avoid such people.

—2 Timothy 3:1–5

♓ PISCES

Pisces, the twelfth and last sign of the zodiac, corresponds to the Twelfth House in the archetype. It is a double-bodied, mutable sign. Pisces represents the highest degree of evolution, because it is the sign of love and compassion. Understanding creates compassion.

The pathway to love is through forgiveness.

—Anonymous

Pisces is the best sign for the spiritually evolved person. While Pisceans often are helpful to others, they are inclined to bring misfortunes upon themselves. Pisces is the sign of suffering. According to Theosophy, the highest evolution can be achieved only through great suffering.

The co-rulers of Pisces are Jupiter and Neptune. Venus is exalted in Pisces. Mercury is in fall and in detriment in this sign. (With Mercury in Pisces, one cannot see reality, only images.) The Moon and Mars are in honour of triplicity, and Saturn and the Sun are peregrine there.

The Pisces ascendant indicates a complex, compassionate nature, which is especially good for psychologists and psychiatrists. It gives a tremendous sensitivity, enabling one to attune to higher forces.

The sign of Pisces can be the most dangerous of all the signs, because it brings illusions. Piscean values are not practical. (Aleister Crowley had his Moon in Pisces, not connected by aspect to his Sun in Leo.)

Pisces is a Jupiterian sign, but it cannot develop without a good Aquarius. Pisces represents the fishes, which have no defence. They swim in opposite directions. Consciousness is missing in Pisces. That is why the Twelfth House, which is connected with Pisces in the archetype, is also the house of sleep, where there is no consciousness.

Sleep is that modification of the mind, which ensues upon the quittance of all objects by the mind, by reason of all waking senses and faculties sinking into abeyance.

—Patanjali, Book I:10

97

For God has not destined us for wrath, but to obtain salvation through our Lord Jesus Christ, Who died for us so that we, whether we wake or sleep, might live with Him.

—1 Thessalonians 5:9–11

For spiritual evolution, it is good to have Jupiter and Venus in Pisces.

The emotions of the Piscean take away his wisdom; everything becomes love. He feels that love cures everything.

Pisces is connected with a very compassionate love. Nurses excel when Pisces is powerful in their charts.

Love thy neighbour as thyself.

—Luke 10:27, Luke 10:36,37

Hatred stirs up strife but love covers all offenses.

—Proverbs of Solomon 10:12

Love

Love is patient and kind; love is not jealous or boastful; it is not arrogant or rude. Love does not insist on its own way; it is not irritable or resentful; it does not rejoice at wrong, but rejoices in the right. Love bears all things, hopes all things, endures all things.

—1 Corinthians 13:4

For I have derived much joy and comfort from your love, my brother, because the hearts of the saints have been refreshed through you.

—Philemon 7

The best sign for Saturn to be in is Pisces, since Saturn would develop the protective quality of Jupiter and the evolved love of Neptune there.

Because you have kept my word of patient endurance, I will keep you from the hour of trial which is coming on the whole world, to try those who dwell upon the earth.

—Revelation 3:10

Blessed is the man who endures trial for when he has stood the test he will receive the crown of life which God has promised to those who love Him.

—James 1:92

Neptune in Pisces can cause too much illusion.

In spiritual circles, it is said that when a human being is connected with a powerful Pisces and does not have the desire to come back to the material plane, it indicates that he has achieved the circle of incarnations.

He who has thrown off the fetters and freed himself in all ways, he is free from sorrow; for him there is no suffering; he has completed his journey.

—The Dhammapada: The Sage 1(90)

Him I call a Brahamana who knows his former lives, who knows heaven and hell, who has reached the end of births, who is a sage of perfect knowledge and who has accomplished all that has to be accomplished.

—The Dhammapada: The Brahamana 41(423)

Another of the disciples said to Him, "Lord, let me first go and bury my father." But Jesus said to him, "Follow me and leave the dead to bury their own dead."

—Matthew 8:21–22

Be free from the future; be free of the past; be free in the present; cross to the younger shore, with a mind wholly free you will not fall into birth and death.

—The Dhammapada: Craving 15(348)

Him I call a Brahamana who is free from anger, devoted to duties, practices divine virtues, who is without craving and controlled. He wears his last body.

—The Dhammapada: The Brahamana 21(403)

The twentieth century is the very end of the Piscean Age.

The Houses

When studying a horoscope, one must study not only the planetary influences, but also the houses. The signs on the cusps of the houses should be compared with the signs on the cusps of the houses in the archetype. Great mistakes in life are caused by a bad aspect between different houses.

The houses considered unfavourable, or negative, are the houses that are not connected with the ascendant by an aspect. These are the Sixth, Eighth, and Twelfth houses. It is best not to have any planets in these houses.

According to some astrologers, the Second House is also unfavourable because it is the house opposite the Eighth and is, therefore, influenced by opposition. The Second House, as the house of gains, has the tendency, especially in these times, to be connected with greed.

> Take heed, and beware of all covetousness; for a man's life does not consist in the abundance of his possessions.
>
> —Luke 12:15

A favourable house is sometimes referred to as a "Hyleg," which means 'life-giver.' An unfavourable house is sometimes referred to as an "anaraeta" (ANAIPETHS), which means 'destroyer of life.'

According to some astrologers, either the Sun (in the case of a man) or the moon (in the case of a woman) should be in a hylegiacal house: 1, 5, 7, 9, 10, or 11. If it is not in such a house, the ascendant becomes the hyleg.

Within this context, houses that would be considered favourable (hylegiacal houses), but only in connection with a specific horoscope are: the First (representing the physical and mental constitution), the Fifth (representing the children and love life), the Seventh (representing partners and marriage), the Ninth (representing higher knowledge), the Tenth (representing one's career and destiny), and the Eleventh (representing friends and hopes and wishes).

For the Third House and the Fourth House, which are not qualified as hylegiacal houses, whether they will be considered as favourable will depend only upon the birth chart of the native under examination.

The houses on the eastern half of the horoscope are most strongly connected with the native. The houses on the western half of the horoscope are most strongly connected with other people. When the majority of the planets are in western houses, the native must give out more than he takes in, and he will have a tremendous need to be connected with other people.

Never study a house without the triplicity to which it belongs.

The influence of a house begins 5 degrees before its cusp and ends 5 degrees from the following house cusp.

The influence of a planet posited in a house will be manifested on the physical level. A planet positioned 5 degrees before the cusp of a house will influence that next house only on a psychological level, as already stated.

It is not of primary importance whether a horoscope is destructive or constructive in its nature. What is of primary importance is if the horoscope is powerful as determined by the signs on the cusps of the angular houses. The first judgement must be about the degree of strength of the horoscope. A weak horoscope makes the native unable to fight his destiny.

The signs on the cusps of the Second, Third, and Fourth House are influential during the last part of a person's life.

In terms of quantity, a planet has an influence of 100 percent when posited in an angular house, 50 percent when posited in a succedent house, and 25 percent when posited in a cadent house. (The exception to this is the Ninth House, which, although cadent, has an influence of 75 percent due to its being next to the mid-heaven.) Thus, the most powerful houses are the Tenth, the Fourth, the First, and the Seventh, followed by the Ninth.

There are certain human beings who are protected. Basically, this could be indicated by one or more of the following: a good ascendant, no planets in the disadvantageous houses (Sixth, Eighth, and Twelfth), Jupiter in the Tenth House (house of destiny), and a good aspect between the Sun and Jupiter, or between the latter and the Sun and the ascendant or the mid-heaven.

Derivated Houses

One needs a tremendous fantasy in order to work with derivations.

With derivations, each house is both a cause and an effect. Derivations permit greater insight to the astrologer.

With derivated houses, the house previous to the one in question is always the house of the secret enemies, and the house following the house in question is always the house of gains. The house ten houses away (the Tenth House) from the house in question is the house of realization. Example: the First House in a horoscope is the realization of the Fourth House. In other words, the native is the product of his parents (or country). Example: the Tenth House is the realization of the First House. In other words, the native's career/destiny is brought about through his physical and mental constitution. Example: the Seventh House is the realization of the Tenth House. In other words, a person may obtain a life partner through his profession. Example: the Fourth House is the realization of the Seventh House. In other words, marriage will produce a home.

If the Ninth House is good, e.g., if there are no hidden enemies there, if one's higher knowledge is not perverted, and if one has not misused his experience in foreign countries, the Tenth House will gain, and as a result, the Eleventh House, being the Second House of the Tenth, will also bring a gain to a good Tenth House,which itself is the gain of higher knowledge.

Trust in the Lord with all your heart, and do not rely on your own insight. In all your ways acknowledge Him and He will make straight your paths.

—Proverbs 3:5,6

First House

Mars is the natural ruler of the First House.

The First House is the most important house because it is the house of the physical and mental constitution of the native. It is interesting to note that the First House is not connected by aspect with the Second (the house of money), the Sixth (the house of short sicknesses, work, and service), the Eighth (the house of death) or the Twelfth (the house of hospitals and prisons). It is considered undesirable for the ruler of the ascendant to be posited in any of these houses, since there would be no aspect between the ascendant and its ruler.

Among the three schools of psychoanalysis, that of Adler, which gives priority to the personality, is connected to the First House.

The less evolved a person is, the more he is under the influence of the houses.

The more evolved a person is, the less he is governed by the houses (with the exception of the First House, which is the signature of his present incarnation). He will be simply under the influence of the signs. In the case of an evolved individual, the houses (with the exception of the First) can be changed during a lifetime through psychogenic training—by freeing oneself from physical, mental, and emotional problems. The houses are around the earth. What you achieve depends upon the ascendant. The more evolved you are, the more you integrate time.

One cannot hope to transcend one's time and to be better than one's time; all one can aspire to is to become one's time at its best.

—Hegel

With the Sun in the same sign as the rising sign, the constitution will be stronger. The Sun increases one's physical strength, and, if posited in the First House, it indicates a tremendous will, due not only to its position in an angular house, but also to its being the ruler of the First House of the archetype (Aries) by exaltation.

Uranus in the First House may produce a very unusual personality. Neptune in the First House may produce a clairvoyant personality.

Second House

Venus is the ruler of the Second House in the archetype. The Second House is the house of money earned through one's own efforts and of all material wealth. If the sign on the cusp of the Second House is a fixed sign, and its ruler is in a good zodiacal state, it will be favourable for making money, especially if the ruler is well aspected.

Through derivation, one can see that one needs money in order to have friends (the Eleventh House is the effect of the Second, the cause). Vice versa, one can see that in order to make life pleasant, one needs money.

Wealth brings many new friends, but a poor man is deserted by his friends.

—Proverbs 19:4

Even my bosom friend in whom I trusted, who ate of my bread, has lifted his heel against me.
—Psalm 41:9

In order to become wise, you must have money and you must work for other people.

A good man leaves an inheritance to his children's children.

—Proverbs 13:22

Bear ye one another's burdens.
—Colossians 3:3

Money comes from the earth. The sign belonging to the Second House in the archetype is Taurus, an earth sign.

According to Adam Smith, the economist of the second half of the eighteenth century, it is our vanity, our desire to be noticed and accepted by others, that motivates us to acquire wealth and material goods.

Be not anxious for goods unjustly gotten; for they shall not profit thee in the day of calamity and revenge.

—Ecclesiasticus V:10

Saturn in the Second House may either bring tremendous wealth or extreme poverty.

Wealth hastily gotten will dwindle but he who gathers little by little will increase it.

—Proverbs 13:11

Third House

The sign on the cusp of the Third House in the archetype is Gemini, ruled by Mercury. The Third House is a weak house because it is a cadent house.

Neighbours and relatives belong to the Third House, as well as schools, communications, technology, and short journeys.

The Third House is the house of the intellect, of rational thinking, of learning, teaching, and, nowadays, of technology. Technology can be seen in the Third House, according to the country and the environment in which the native lives. The advance of technology works against Saturn (the planet of time, of fate, and of destiny).

104

With a good Third House well-connected with the Ninth, one's intelligence can evolve into wisdom.

To watch the mind is conducive to happiness.

—The Dhammapada: The Mind 4:36

Apply your mind to instruction and your ears to words of knowledge.

—Proverbs 23:12

On the lips of him who has understanding wisdom is found.

—Proverbs 10:13

Intelligence means to see what is worthwhile seeing.

The purpose in a man's mind is like dry water, but a man of understanding will draw it out.

—Proverbs 20:5

The right thinking will enable you to escape the suffering of the Twelfth House. One can be trained to be more rational, but such training will be made easier if the environment (educational opportunities, etc.) is propitious.

Practical intelligence is lacking when Mercury is in detriment or in fall.

Intelligence has a secret enemy: money. Thus, the secret enemy of the Third House is the Second House. One way to overcome the negative influence of money would be to buy (and read) books.

When forming a judgement about a person's intelligence, one should look to see if there is a connection between the person's Uranus and Mercury. If Uranus is in a good aspect with Mercury, the person will have a very quick mind.

According to Patanjali (the Indian Yogi of the second century A.D.), purification of the mind is achieved by practicing benevolence, tenderness, and complacency.

Mercury in Capricorn in the Third House imparts a serious nature to the affairs of the Third House.

We know that one's vitality can be improved. Can intelligence serve to prolong one's life?

Many are the plans in the mind of man but it is the purpose of the Lord that will be established.

—Proverbs 17:21

For man does not know his time. Like fish which are taken in an evil net, and like birds which are caught in a snare, so the sons of men are snared at an evil time, when it suddenly falls upon them.

—Ecclesiastes 9:12

Not in the sky, not in the depths of the sea, nor in mountain cliffs is there a place on earth where a man can be and death cannot overcome him.

—The Dhammapada: Evil Conduct 13(128)

No man has power to retain the spirit or authority over the day of death.

—Ecclesiastes 8:8

By endeavour, by vigilance, by discipline and self-control, let the wise man make for himself an island which no flood can overwhelm.

—The Dhammapada: Vigilance 5(25)

In the path of righteousness is life, but the way of error leads to death.

—Proverbs 12:28

He who keeps the commandments keeps his life: he who despises the word will die.

—Proverbs 20:16

The fear of the Lord prolongs life, but the years of the wicked will be short.

—Proverbs 10:27

Riches do not profit in the day of wrath, but righteousness delivers from death.

—Proverbs 10:27

The highway of the upright turns aside from evil: he who guards his way preserves his life.

—Proverbs 16:17

The Third House, as stated previously, is also the house of neighbours.

He who belittles his neighbour lacks sense, but a man of understanding remains silent.

—Proverbs 11:12

Argue your case with your neighbour himself, and do not disclose another's secret.

—Proverbs 25:9

Do not say to your neighbour, "Go and come again, tomorrow I will give it," when you have it with you.

—Proverbs 3:26

We who are strong ought to bear with the failings of the weak, and not to please ourselves: let each of us please his neighbour for his good to edify him.

—Romans 15:1

Do not neglect to show hospitality to strangers, for thereby some have entertained angels unaware.

—Hebrews 13:1–2

Fourth House

The Fourth House in the archetype is connected with the sign of Cancer, in which the Moon rules and Jupiter is exalted.

The Fourth House is the house of the parents, the genes, the home, the emotions, and the unconscious. It shows the circumstances surrounding the beginning and end of life. It is one of the most influential houses, being fourth in importance after the First, the Tenth, and the Seventh houses.

To determine if a horoscope is that of a healer, we have to study the First House (physical and mental constitution), the Third House (intelligence), and the Fourth House. The true healer is greatly connected with the Fourth House and the Moon.

When analyzing a horoscope, one of the first things one should examine, besides the ascendant, is the Fourth House.

When trying to solve a problem in a horoscope, look at the Fourth House (the house of genes) because a person is the product of his parents, and the problem may be due to his upbringing.

Happiness depends a lot on one's Fourth House. (In the archetype, Jupiter is exalted there.) It is best for a child to be born from healthy parents and at a favourable hour. Happiness must start in the family.

A good Fourth House provides good parents and thus healthy genes, as well as a happy beginning and end of life. The happiness or unhappiness of children depends greatly on their parents.

Train up a child in the way he should go and when he is old he will not depart from it.

—Proverbs 22:6

The worst thing a parent can do is to push a child to strive for material security.

A righteous man who walks in his integrity blessed are his sons after him!

—Proverbs 20:7

A bad planet in the Fourth House causes misfortunes.

An evolved person should aim at the best possible cooperation between the Fourth and the Tenth Houses (parents and profession).

One's mental inheritance is shown through the Fourth House.

It is important for one's horoscope to be well connected with those of one's parents. One's first house (representing the mental and physical constitution) is the Tenth House (the realization) of the Fourth House (representing the beginning and the end of life). In other words, you are the product of your parents. The Fourth House is also the significator of the parent of the same sex as the native, while the Tenth House is the significator of the parent of the opposite sex.

Grandchildren are the crown of the aged, and glory of sons is their fathers.

—Proverbs 17:6

A stellium (four or more planets in one sign) in a sign other than the sign on the ascendant will be more influential than the interference from one's parents (Fourth House), but in such a case, the horoscope will lack harmony. Therefore, strength will be needed in order to take the disharmony and use it as a drive. Never judge a horoscope without looking at the Fourth House, from which you know the native's environment.

With Gemini (a mutable sign) in the Fourth House, one's values will be very superficial and changeable.

If the Moon is in the Fourth House and is opposed by Saturn, the unconscious will be repressed.

Uranus and Saturn in the Fourth House produce difficulties, Saturn being the enemy of happiness and Uranus standing for instability.

Fifth House

The Sun is the ruler of the Fifth House in the archetype.

The Fifth House is the house of love, pleasure, hobbies, the arts, entertainment, and children. It is also the house of bars and of money obtained through speculation and laws of chance. It is the house of realization of the Eighth House (sex drive). The Second House is the tenth (the realization, the effect) of the Fifth House.

Of the three schools of psychoanalysis, those of Freud, Jung, and Adler, it is Freud who emphasizes the Fifth House.

An actor/actress should have good Fifth and Seventh (the public) houses. Publicity is very expensive, so an actor/actress must be able to gain exposure through social life. An actor/actress must be ruthless due to tremendous competition and must not be too emotional or sensitive so as not to be affected too strongly by negative criticism.

Saturn in the Fifth House often indicates childlessness.

Uranus in the Fifth House often indicates homosexuality.

Neptune in the Fifth House can produce a lack of reality and may give a very strange approach to love.

In the chart of a physician, if the ruler of the Tenth House is in the Fifth House, he may be involved with pediatrics.

Sixth House

Mercury is the ruler of Virgo, the sign on the cusp of the Sixth House in the archetype.

The Sixth House is the house of work, service, and short sicknesses which develop quickly and which last less than 27⅓ days (a lunar revolution).

> A cheerful heart is a good medicine but a downcast spirit dries up the bones.
>
> —Proverbs 17:22

The Sixth House also represents the working class, the underprivileged in society, and employees.

In order to serve others well, one must have a good Fifth as well as Sixth House. Why do we mention the Fifth? Because too many problems from children and/or an excess of physical love and pleasure can interfere in one's service to others. In such a case, the Fifth House becomes the enemy of the Sixth.

If the ruler of the First House is in the Sixth House, it is considered undesirable, since the First House is not connected with the Sixth House by aspect. The Sixth House, with its subordinate position, is not an advantageous house for the native. An exception would be if the native is working as a physician or for the underprivileged classes.

> Do not withhold good from those to whom it is due when it is in your power to do it.
>
> —Proverbs 3:27

> Do not delay when the matter is unpleasant.
>
> —Ecclesiastes 8:8

> Those who live in the pleasure-ground of fancy see truth in the unreal and untruth in the real. They never arrive at truth.
>
> —The Dhammapada: The Twin Verses I(11)

For a successful career, the Tenth, the Second, and the Sixth houses must all be good. In order to work, you need tools. If you misuse your tools, you will be unable to work. One tool is your physical body. Sicknesses come from shortcomings in the intelligence of people.

> Health is the greatest of gifts.
>
> —The Dhammapada: Happiness 15(204)

Pleasant words are like honeycomb, sweetness to the soul and health to the body.

—Proverbs 16:27

Against all sicknesses there is a cure in the forest.

—Paracelsus

Seventh House

Venus is the ruler of the Seventh House, which is connected with the sign of Libra in the archetype. It is the house of the alter ego, of marriage, partnership, the public and open enemies. (Hidden enemies are in the Twelfth House.)

You are lucky if you have a good Seventh House.

One must not isolate oneself from other people.

Marriage partners (as well as business partners) can become open enemies. Therefore, one must use a lot of foresight in choosing one's life partner, in order to choose the right one.

House and wealth are inherited from fathers, but a prudent wife from the Lord.

—Proverbs 19:34

He who finds a wife finds a good thing, and obtains favour from the Lord.

—Proverbs 18:22

A good wife is the crown of her husband, but she who brings shame is like rottenness in his bones.

—Proverbs 12:4

Depart not from a wise and good wife, whom thou hast gotten in the fear of the Lord; for the grace of her modesty is above gold.

—Ecclesiasticus VII:21

When, in a woman's chart, the ruler of the Seventh House is in the Twelfth, it means that the husband will have a sickness and/or be a secret enemy. The sixth house from the seventh is the twelfth, and a sickness connected with the Seventh House (the house of marriage and partners) will become a hidden "enemy" for the native.

111

In horary astrology, the astrologer is represented by the Seventh House.

In order to find out about one's friends, one must look at the eleventh house of one's horoscope, but the third and the seventh houses must be well connected. Bad friends can destroy one's values, and they may prevent the full development of the potentials of one's ascending sign, since one may simply become their servant. By derivation, the Third House is the Ninth House of the Seventh. Thus, if the third house is bad, it means that the partners will lack wisdom.

He who walks with wise men becomes wise, but the companion of fools will suffer harm.

—Proverbs 13:20

There are friends who pretend to be friends, but there is a friend who sticks closer than a brother.

—Proverbs 18:24

He who consorts with fools experiences grief. The company of fools is like the company of enemies—productive of pain. Company of the wise is like meeting of real kinsfolk—it brings happiness.

—The Dhammapada: Happiness 11(207)

Eighth House

Mars and Pluto are the natural co-rulers of the Eighth House. Mars is in its night domicile in Scorpio, the sign belonging to the Eighth House in the archetype.

The Eighth House is the house of death, surgery, money received from others (via inheritance or otherwise), and regeneration through the sex drive. (We regenerate in our children.)

The survival of the race depends upon Scorpio.

Sexuality is needed for an optimistic attitude in life, but sexuality takes away wisdom—it is a secret enemy of the Ninth House (the house of wisdom and higher knowledge). The moment sex enters, wisdom departs.

The Sun in the Eighth House can indicate death in a public place, or a death that is publicized.

Jupiter in a good zodiacal state in the Eighth House can indicate an easy death, money from other people, and inheritance.

Saturn in the Eighth House can cause a long sickness and a slow death, with much suffering, or death through a fall.

Ninth House

Jupiter is the ruler of the Ninth House, which is sometimes called the House of God.

> The Lord is my chosen portion and my cusp;
> Thou holdest my lot
> The lines have fallen for me in pleasant places
> Yes, I have a goodly heritage.
>
> —Psalm 16:5–6

The sign of Sagittarius is on the cusp of the Ninth House in the archetype. It is associated with higher knowledge, wisdom, and spiritual approaches to life, religion, dreams, long journeys, and foreign countries. Higher knowledge has also to do with foreign countries. According to a German saying, "if God loves you, he sends you to foreign countries."

> Virtue lasting in old age is happiness,
> Faith firmly rooted is happiness,
> Attainment of wisdom is happiness,
> Avoidance of sins is happiness.
>
> —The Dhammapada:
> The Elephant 14(333)

> I bless the Lord who gives me counsel;
> In the night also my heart instructs me.
>
> —Psalm 16:7

By dwelling on knowledge that presents itself in a dream, steadiness of mind may be produced.

> —Patanjali, Book I:38

Jungian psychology places an emphasis on the Ninth House.

By bringing to one's consciousness one's dreams, future bad events can more easily be escaped.

If the ruler of the Fourth House is in the Ninth House, it is likely that one will make his home in a foreign country.

If the ruler of the Ninth House is also the ruler of the Tenth, it is excellent, since it will bring wisdom into the destiny of the native.

The Ninth House should not be connected with the planet Mercury, because no good aspect exists in the archetype between Mercury and Jupiter, the ruler of the Ninth House in the archetype. The signs of Mercury cannot be in good aspect with the signs of Jupiter. As stated previously, Mercury in the Ninth House in detriment is unfavourable for metaphysics.

Neptune in the Ninth House may provide an interest in metaphysics and a mystical approach to religion. If it is in a watery sign, it will be very influential and mediumistic.

Wisdom is achieved through will power and patience:

He is called an elder in whom dwells truth, virtue, non-violence, restraint and control and who is free from impurity and is wise.

—The Dhammapada: One Established in Law 6(261)

Train yourself in godliness for while bodily training is of some value, godliness is of value in every way, as it holds promise for the present life and also for the life to come. The saying is sure and worthy of full acceptance. For to this end we toil and strive because we have our hope set on the living God, who is the Saviour of all men, especially of those who believe.

—1 Timothy 4:7

And he said to man, "I behold, the fear of the Lord, that is wisdom and to depart from evil is understanding."

—Proverbs

The beginning of wisdom is this: Get wisdom and whatever you get, get insight. Prize her highly and she will exalt you. She will honour you if you embrace her.

—Proverbs 4:7,8

If any of you lacks wisdom, let him ask God, who gives to all men generously and without reproaching, and it will be given him. But let him ask in faith, with no doubting, for he who doubts is like a wave of the sea that is driven and tossed by the wind. For that person must not suppose that a double-minded man, unstable in all his ways, will receive anything from the Lord.

—James 1:5,6,7,8

As an example of sufferings and patience, brethren take the prophets who spoke in the name of the Lord. Behold, we call those happy who were steadfast. You have heard of the steadfastness of Job, and you have seen the purpose of the Lord, how the Lord is compassionate and merciful.

—James 5:11

He is wise and righteous who guides others not by force and violence but equitably. He is the guardian of the law.

—The Dhammapada: One Established in Law 2(257)

Wise men lay up knowledge.

—Proverbs 10:14

Give instruction to a wise man and he will be still wiser: teach a righteous man and he will increase in learning. The fear of the Lord is the beginning of wisdom, and the knowledge of the Holy One is insight.

—Proverbs 9:9,10

Tenth House

Saturn is the ruler of Capricorn, the sign belonging to the Tenth House in the archetype. The Tenth House is the house of the future, of destiny, and of time. It is also the house connected with the career, responsibility, and honours. One's life is realized through the Tenth House. Thus, a person's drive should go to the Tenth House.

Do not delay when the matter is unpleasant.

—Ecclesiastes 8:8

A good profession is the best solution for happiness.

Whenever you look at a specific house, never forget that it is the tenth house of another house, and that its meaning must be combined with that of the other house.

A person who wishes to evolve must aim at the best possible cooperation between the Fourth and Tenth houses (home and profession).

One's profession, as signified by the Tenth House, ideally should be connected with a cardinal sign (Aries, Cancer, Libra, Capricorn).

In order to have a successful career, a harmonious aspect is needed between the Tenth, the Second (money), and the Sixth (employees, health) houses. The equilateral triangle formed by the cusps of the Tenth, the Second, and the Sixth Houses in the archetype is represented symbolically by the upper triangle in the Seal of Solomon.

The Tenth House is connected with leadership.

When the ruler of the ascendant is in the Tenth House, the native will be inclined to overestimate himself and will take his future into his own hands. If the ruler of the ascendant is the Sun, and it is in the Tenth, there will be a drive for leadership. The Sun in Aries in the Tenth, even when it is not the ruler of the ascendant, will also give a drive for leadership.

The Tenth House signifies the parent of the sex opposite that of the native.

Saturn in the Tenth House is not good. At best it brings foresight. "You will not escape from that of which you are afraid." However, people who have Saturn in the Tenth House are connected with their professions very seriously. An inferiority complex can cause one to work too hard.

The Tenth House should not be connected with the emotions (watery signs). One must be patient in connection with his future.

Hope deferred makes the heart sick, but a desire fulfilled is a tree of life.

—Proverbs 13:12

When, in a horoscope, the mid-heaven (or the ascendant) by direction forms an aspect with a planet, the destiny of the native will be influenced according to the nature of the planet, the sign, and the house in which the planet is.

Any honours a person may receive are shown by the Tenth House. You cannot give yourself honours; they are given to you by others. Leadership is conferred. What is important is not he who preaches, but those who listen.

One does not get power from oneself, but from others.

It is like sport to a fool to do wrong but wise conduct is pleasure to a man of understanding.

—Proverbs 10:23

He who walks in integrity walks securely, but he who perverts his ways
will be found out.

—Proverbs 10:9

Blessed are those who hunger and thirst for righteousness, for they shall
be satisfied.

Blessed are those who are persecuted for righteousness' sake, for theirs is
the Kingdom of Heaven.

—Matthew 5:6,10

He who by his good deeds transforms his evil acts is like the moon when
free from a cloud.

—The Dhammapada: The World 7(173)

Eleventh House

The Eleventh House is the house of friends, good luck (bona fortuna), and hopes and wishes.

Saturn and Uranus are the co-rulers of the Eleventh House in the
archetype. Aquarius is the sign belonging to the Eleventh House.

Good luck depend upon how one reacts and how one receives
planetary influences.

Every good endowment and every perfect gift is from above, coming down
from the Father of lights with whom there is no variation of shadow due
to change.

—James 1:16–17

Friends must be stable and communicate in a humanitarian way.
People who love you should be intelligent.

A friend loves at all times, and a brother is born for adversity.

—Proverbs 17:174

Saturn in the Eleventh House indicates elderly people as friends.

117

The Sun in the Eleventh House indicates very influential, prominent friends.

If we derivate, the Eleventh House is the second of the tenth; in other words, it represents the money made by one's employer, if we take the Tenth House to be the employer. Therefore, if the Eleventh House is bad, then one's employer may not be good from the point of view of giving you money.

Friends ill-chosen may become hidden enemies, an example of how the proceeding house, in this case the Twelfth, is the gain of the preceding one.

> He who walks with wise men becomes wise, but the companion of fools will suffer harm.
>
> —Proverbs 13:20

> Do not be friends with evil doers or of mean men, do be friends with the good; keep company with the best of men.
>
> —The Dhammapada: The Wise Man 3(79)

A good Eleventh House is advantageous for the affairs of the Twelfth House.

Twelfth House

The Twelfth House is connected with suffering, jails, chronic sicknesses, self-undoing, hospitals and institutions, sleep, misfortunes, hidden or secret enemies. In a general way, the Twelfth House is always connected with undesirable things.

> Misfortune pursues sinners, but prosperity rewards the righteous.
>
> —Proverbs 13:21

> Avoidance of sins is happiness.
>
> —The Dhammapada: The Elephant 14(333)

> He who closes his mouth preserves his life, he who opens wide his lips comes to ruin.
>
> —Proverbs 13:3

He who offends the harmless and the innocent soon reaches one of these
ten states: He will suffer (1) sharp pain or (2) disease or (3) bodily decay
or (4) grievous disaster or (5) loss of mind or (6) displeasure of the King or
(7) calumny or (8) loss of relations or (9) loss of all his wealth or (10)
destruction of his house by lightning or fire. At death, poor fool, he finds
rebirth in woe.

—The Dhammapada: The Rod of Punishment 9–12 (137–140)

Jupiter and Neptune are the co-rulers of the Twelfth House, which
is connected with Pisces in the archetype.

Neptune posited in the Twelfth House can be too powerful, since it
is already a co-ruler of that house in the archetype.

The weakest of all the houses is the Twelfth House. A person with
too many planets in the Twelfth House will not easily get recognition.
When there are no planets in the Twelfth House, it shows that there are
no hidden enemies.

The planets in the Twelfth House can influence the ascendant,
depending upon their orbs.

The Twelfth House is also connected with metaphysics and the
occult. An excellent Twelfth House is advantageous for spiritual evolution, but the Twelfth House can bring tremendous misfortunes for the
unevolved person. The advantages of the Twelfth House are usually
ignored by most astrologers, who focus only on the disadvantages.

If we live by the Spirit, let us also walk by the Spirit. Let us have no
self-conceit, no provoking of one another, no envy of one another.

—Galatians 5:18–26

When a man's ways please the Lord, he makes even his enemies to be at
peace with him.

—Proverbs 16:7

Better to be wronged than to do wrong.

—Socrates

If, in a horoscope, the ruler of the Ninth House is in the Twelfth,
the native will have a strong interest in metaphysics.

The Bible is the best book to read in order to help sicknesses
connected with the Twelfth House: pray and work—"ora et labora."

And the prayer of faith will save the sick man and the Lord will raise him up; and if he has committed sins (self-undoing), he will be forgiven.

—James 5:15

For everyone who calls upon the name of the Lord will be saved.

—Romans 10:13

In the chart of a physician, the ruler of the Tenth House may be in the Twelfth House.

If a sickness lasts more than 27⅓ days (one lunar month), it becomes chronic and belongs to the Twelfth House.

A man's spirit will endure sickness, but a broken spirit who can bear.

—Proverbs 18:14

If we derivate, the Twelfth House is the eighth (the house of death) of the Fifth (the house of love and children). The death of one's children would cause tremendous suffering.

The Twelfth House, as a derivated house, is the realization (the Tenth House) of the Third House, the Third House being the cause and the Twelfth House the effect. The Twelfth House will reflect the effects of one's rational thinking. If you have the right thinking (i.e., a good Third House), you will not have sufferings caused by the Twelfth House.

The more civilized the country is in which you live, the more rational you will most likely be. Therefore, how rational or irrational someone is depends not only upon the horoscope, but also on factors beyond the horoscope.

A good Twelfth House can be achieved by improving one's Eleventh House. By way of derivation, the Twelfth House is the Sixth House (the house of work or service) of the Seventh (others). It is also the house of gains (the Second) of the Eleventh, indicating how much money your friends have.

We who are strong ought to bear with the failings of the weak, and not to please ourselves: Let each of us please his neighbour for his good, to edify him.

—Romans 15:1

According to Theosophists, if you want to understand the Twelfth

120

House fully, you must believe in karma and reincarnation. The purpose of incarnation is to evolve and to render services to others. It is also said that an incarnation reflects the battle between the ego and the higher self. The aim must be to learn to live in harmony with others, and to identify oneself with other creatures through tolerance, understanding, benevolence, and compassion. Understanding brings compassion.

> All people hold him dear who has both virtue and insight, who is established in the law, who is truthful, and fulfills his own karma.
>
> —The Dhammapada: The Pleasant 9(217)

One must have an altruistic attitude in order to help one's fellow men and to assist them in discovering the truth with which they can "decipher" the seven seals (the book of nature with the seven planets).

> And I saw in the right hand of him who was seated on the throne a scroll written within and on the back, sealed with seven seals;
>
> —Revelation 5:1

> As for the mystery of the seven stars which you saw in my right hand and the seven golden lampstands, the seven stars are the angels of the seven churches and the seven lampstands are the seven churches.
>
> —Revelation 1:20

> And we exhort you, brethren, admonish the idle, encourage the fainthearted, help the weak, be patient with them all.
>
> —1 Thessalonians 5:14

In the present state of civilization, the consciousness of people is clouded by desire, and thus we can have only a partial perception of the meaning of life and evolution.

> "Child of the day!" answered Zanoni, mournfully, "have I not told thee the error of our knowledge was forgetfulness of the desires and passions which the spirit never can wholly and permanently conquer, while this matter cloaks it?"
>
> —*Zanoni*
> Sir Edward Bulwer Lytton

Error in our perception prevails, owing to conflicting desires, goals, and interests on the individual, ethnic, national, and religious levels. Wisdom is knowledge, free from error.

> In common with thy race, it must be thine to suffer to struggle and to err. But mild be thy human trials, and strong be thy spirit, to love and to believe.
>
> —*Zanoni*
> Sir Edward Bulwer Lytton

As long as we stick to earthly values, too much knowledge can lead us to unhappiness, because earthly values can easily lead to error.

The key to wisdom and harmony is found in the power of intuition. Intuition is the voice of conscience, which leads us to wisdom by opening our senses and attuning us to higher forces, thus increasing the power of the conscious, in order to influence the unconscious in the right direction. We tend to avoid considering the existence of higher beings because generally we are not evolved enough to understand them.

We lack the clarity necessary to bring to our consciousness the illumination of dreams.

> Do not quench the spirit, do not despise prophesying, but test everything.
>
> —1 Thessalonians 5:19,20

In our own countries, the symbols with which we are consciously or unconsciously connected, reflect a specific civilization. According to the Theosophists, we have to keep the secrets until the Masters decide that they can be revealed.

The meaning of underlying allegories (the signs of the Zodiac) appeal to the heart and can lead us on the path to wisdom, thus bringing us peace of mind and keeping us away from anxiety, which results from ignorance.

The use of allegories was a practice of all rabbinical schools and was also followed by Jesus.

> I will open my mouth in a parable;
> I will utter dark sayings from of old,
> things that we have heard and known,
> that our fathers have told us.
> We will not hide them from their children,
> but tell to the coming generation
> the glorious deeds of the Lord and his might
> and the wonders which he has wrought.
>
> —Psalm 78:2

The Twelfth House, because of its association in the archetype with Pisces, is the house of compassion. It is also the house of past lives. A person with no planets in the Twelfth House will not have to pay a karmic debt. Bad planets there show a karmic debt—you will have to pay for mistakes made in previous incarnations. Good planets in a good zodiacal state in the Twelfth House enable the native to help other people to pay for their karmic debts. With planets in a bad zodiacal state in the Twelfth House, one's own karmic debt may be increased.

When the ruler of one's ascendant is in the Twelfth House, one should look at the rulers of the Twelfth House of the archetype (Jupiter and Neptune), as they appear in one's horoscope, before making a judgement. If the ruler of the ascendant is in detriment in the Twelfth House, the native will have an inferiority complex and a given shyness.

If Saturn is the ruler of the Twelfth House in a horoscope and is bodily in the Fourth House, it could indicate that one of the native's parents might have been wrong, and a secret enemy of the native.

Wherever Saturn is, there is loneliness or unhappiness. Saturn posited in the Fourth House and coming from the Twelfth (the house of bad fortune) will reflect misfortunes for the home and for the beginning and end of life of the native.

Index of Authors, Personalities, and Texts